Pipe Dreams

A Memoir

The life & growth of a man

and a company

By W. Lynn Thomas
As told to LeAnn Thomas

ISBN 978-0-9883806-0-8

Photo Credits: Like It Was/ Kearney Hub, p 61; Kearney Hub, p 123

Pipe Dream:

A fantastic plan, hope or story.

Table of Contents

Preface

I remember asking *my* mother to write down the story of her life. I even bought her a spiral notebook to record her memories. I have only one page about her pleasant memories as a child in Boone, Iowa. I would not like this to happen to my children and grandchildren. And ever since I turned 70 years old, my daughters have been after me to write down my memories. Now that I've turned 87 years old, I guess it's time to put down in words the stories I've told them.

Even though my parents left me no money, they did show me love and care about my future. I lived in a time when some people simply looked on with pity at my challenges and called me that "poor little crippled boy." But I also lived in a time when I could come in contact with so many great people who gave me encouragement to go for it!

And so with no money, no assets, no faculty to walk, I set out with dreams that I could do the impossible, to have children, to build a dream house, to put together a company and a host of employees that would join my dreams. For out of dreams and thought, everything is built and accomplished. Show me a person who has no dreams, and I'll show you a person poor in spirit. Out of our thoughts, all is created.

And for me I had people in my childhood and throughout my life who gave me encouragement and motivation. Let me encourage you: use your ability and motivation to have the wonderful life of your dreams.

Partly, this book is about my experiences growing up with polio. But this is also a story about people. There are many people who have been important to my life, and you will find those people in the pages of this book. And this is a story about growing up in Kearney, Nebraska, a town situated on the north bank of the Platte River and a distance of 1733 miles from Boston and 1733 miles from San Francisco—middle America.

My life has been an interesting ride for me, and I hope you will enjoy the ride as well.

W. Lynn Thomas

"First you creep,
then you walk, then you run.
That's how life goes."

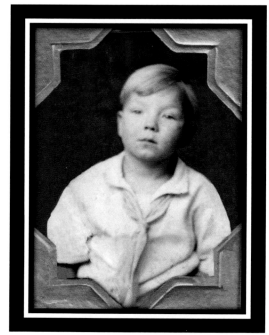

Part 1: The life & growth of a man

To begin: It was 1925 and in some areas around the United States and the world, life popped with the excitement of the Roaring Twenties. For some it was a time of prosperity and dance and expansion. But for some, especially in the rural areas, though, life was always—and continued to be—a physical struggle to meet the most basic needs such as housing and heat and food. My family fell into the last category. Then a few years later with the depression, the struggle worsened into a colorful catastrophe of just making do.

I was born on a farm northeast of Kearney but with a Gibbon address. My mother told me I weighed ten pounds. A midwife, Fern Fish, rode over to the house and delivered me. I was the ninth child of eleven children.

Polio. I was five years old when the weakness and numbing started, and I stayed in bed for a year. The doctor, C.B. Edwards, who was our family doctor, prescribed that I be put to bed and rested, not knowing this was just the opposite thing to do for better healing. Instead, I should've kept active. But it happened and that's the way it was at the time. They didn't know what was wrong with me. They didn't know I had polio.

My muscles just sort of stopped working very well, and as the weeks and months passed my leg and feet muscles became so weak that I couldn't walk. The cords in my legs pulled up on me like draw strings of rubber, pulling tighter and tighter. Conversely, I used my left foot to push myself around in bed, and the strength in that leg partially came back because it got the exercise it needed. Otherwise, I lay in bed for a year before I went to the hospital.

Most doctors really didn't know how to treat polio. That was in 1930. Yet, unbeknown to many, there was a Sister Kenny from Australia who was having success treating polio patients using both physical rehabilitation and hot compresses made from wool blankets. If I had used her methods and gotten more exercise, I would not have been nearly as bad off as I am, but my doctors didn't know. They did the best they could at the time. And that's the way life goes.

At six years old, after one year of lying in bed, Dr. Edwards sent me to the Orthopedic Hospital in Lincoln, Nebraska. It was under the jurisdiction of the Welfare Department of the State of Nebraska, and my parents, being very poor, needed that assistance with my medical needs.

The Welfare paid for my medical help, but they did not provide any financial help for my parents to travel with me to the hospital. And we were just too poor to have money for travel to visit me in Lincoln. So at only six years old the county drivers loaded me up and took me to the Orthopedic Hospital. Feeling alone and lonely, I ached for my family and my home in Kearney.

Living at the hospital, what memories they were! One of the first things they did was put me in what they called a double-spike cast. This was a solid cast that covered both legs and then continued up to the middle of my chest. Then my legs were spread apart with a broomstick between them to keep them solidly apart.

If they'd put me in a pool longer, used hot packs, and exercised me, I would've been a lot better off. But some doctors at that time believed in stabilizing the body. I stayed in that cast for several months, and then they took me out of that and put my legs into braces. One of the braces ran down the right leg with an iron strap that went down and hooked into my shoe and then came up my back and strapped around my chest. On the other leg was what they called a ring caliber brace. This brace has a ring at the top of the brace with attached metal supports running down the length of the leg, so the upper thigh sits in the ring, giving support. I did have strength in my left leg, but they still put a brace on it.

Lincoln hospital again. When I went back to Lincoln Orthopedic Hospital the next year, I spent about 13 months straight in the hospital before I saw my family and my home. I was just eight years old. In 1933 during that long stay at the hospital, my dad was able to visit me once. He rode along with a load of cattle by train to Chicago, and on the train ride back, he got to stop in Lincoln and see me.

How I remember, day after day at the hospital, sitting in my little wagon out by the fence watching the traffic go by and aching to be at home with my parents and my little brother. I don't know, I guess it's been so many years ago for me to remember exactly all the things that went through my young mind, but I do remember I was heartbroken, not having my

3

parents and my little brother with me. This went on for, like I say, 13 months and then the doctors finally sent me home. I was at the hospital off and on from '32 to '37. About every summer I was there at the hospital.

 I missed school during those two years, so that put me behind two years in my education. When I came home they put me in the first grade while other kids my age were in the third grade. Mrs. Lottie Lavington was the teacher. Because it was difficult for me to sit down wearing the braces, they set up a teacher's desk for me so I could stand up and do my homework from there. Everybody treated me very well. I remember the kids in my third grade class, and looking at our class picture I can name every student by their first and last names.

Light Candle, March of Dimes Banquet. In 1935 Howard Nims asked my parents if they would allow him to pick me up and take me to light the candle at the March of Dimes banquet. Howard was the mayor of Kearney at the time, and he also ran a filling station at the corner of 23rd Street and 2nd Avenue.   The banquet was to be held in the old Fort Kearney Hotel in the Crystal Ball Rooms. Mr. Nims picked me up, and I lit a candle at the banquet in the beautiful ballroom. I just remember walking on crutches across the big wooden dance floor and getting to the cake and lighting the candles. When Mr. Nims took me home, he gave a Hershey candy bar to my brother Art and me.

Because it was so difficult for me to sit down wearing the braces, they set up a teacher's desk for me, so I could stand up and do my homework from there. Everybody treated me very well. I remember the kids in my third grade class, and looking at our class picture, I can name every student. I am in the back row wearing a white shirt and overalls.

Third Grade Class Picture:

Front Row: Jerry Jenkins, Wendell, Duane Wolford, Wayne Johnston, Don Slack, Alden Wolford, Billy Tatum.

Second Row: Iris Loebig, Betty Slack, Albert Ingram, Bobby Dye, Hazel Smith, Agnes Walters, Twila, Eddie Bacon, Jean Didricksen, Pauline Martin, Gloria Robinson.

Third Row: Irene Hamblin, Herman Olson, Bula Kersting, Betty Bowker, Wendell Brisban, Herbert Brown, Lorraine Claussen, Bula Paul, Pauline Jacoby, Lynn Thomas, Don Nelson, Clara Sharp.

Teacher: Miss Loti Lavington.

3RD GRADE
11-19-34

MOSS

6

. A. ALCORN, M. D.
SUPERINTENDENT

State of Nebraska

ORTHOPEDIC HOSPITAL
LINCOLN

Jan. 4, 1933.

Mrs. Verner Thomas,
R. R. #4,
Kearney, Nebraska.

Dear Mrs. Thomas:

Lynn is out of his cast and wears splints on his legs. He shows much improvement in his legs but the doctors thought it advisable for him to swim and do exercises a few weeks before he has shoes and braces. He goes swimming every day and also goes to school every day and is doing nicely.

He needs overalls and shirts. As to size you get them for a boy age 12 so there will be plenty of room for shrinkage. He will need shoes too for his brace. We will have him fitted if you can send four dollars for them. It will be a few weeks before he will need the shoes.

Lynn had a nice Christmas. He is well and happy and gaining in weight. He sends you all his love.

Sincerely,

Frieda Penfold R.N.
Supt. of Nurses.

FP:JL

THOMAS FAMILY

At the time of the March of Dimes banquet, we lived at 1822 Ave F in southeast Kearney.

Moving around Kearney. My family moved 13 times in the first 17 years of my life.

We moved from 1822 Avenue F to a triangle wedge of property on Railroad Street and Avenue F, where home would now be under the Avenue H overpass concrete supports. Next we moved to Avenue I and 25th Street, then to the 700 block on 25th Street, and then way up in northwest Kearney to a house on Reservoir Hill. Then we turned around and moved back to 25th Street where Buffalo Motel sits now. We moved and moved and moved again, almost yearly.

We didn't live anywhere very long because we would get behind on our rent and get kicked out, or occasionally we'd move so Dad could be closer to his job. It was very hard times and sometimes Dad couldn't pay the rent. Dad had only an 8th grade education, and in those days you went to work when you finished 8th grade.

Oscar Verner Thomas. My dad, born Oscar Verner Thomas, went by Vern. Dad relished a good cigar, good conversation and a good meal. Dad was a hard worker, never drank any alcohol, but he did love to smoke a cigar. My brother Art and I could always count on candy in Dad's pocket if he could afford a cigar.

His favorite pastime was visiting. I remember as a boy on Saturday afternoons, Dad would take me with him to the Higgins Pool Hall. He would sit and talk and puff on a cigar. Once, my brother Roy said he drove by the corner of 21st and Central Avenue and Dad was talking to someone. Roy drove by two hours later and Dad was still on the same corner visiting.

The nurses wrote notes and letters to my family to let them know of my needs and status. In this letter dated January 4, 1933, the nurse tells my family that I had a nice Christmas at the hospital and other news.

Dad loved to play the fiddle. I remember Dad, Mom, my brother Art and I would take off in our Model T to Buckeye Valley—maybe go to the home of Bob Long, Everett Shiers, Charley Fish, or Winnie Catlin. The revelers would roll up the rug and have an all night dance. Art and I would sleep in the car when we got tired. Dad also played drums and fiddle with Stan Dowers later in his life.

Sometimes on Sundays our family would go up to Everett and Fossie Shiers farm for dinner. And they trained their goat to pull a cart. All us kids would take turns riding in it. Simple times.

For many years Dad worked as a yardman at the Kearney Livestock, which was owned at that time by Earl York, Jud Henline, and Bill McCerney. His pay at that time was seven dollars per week. He was on call at all times of the day. I remember in 1939 he finally got to the amount of 20 dollars per week at Kearney Livestock, and Social Security took 25 cents of that check. For a while he drove truck for Hutchinson Nursery, a nursery that used to be over east of Good Samaritan Hospital. In about 1943 he went to work at the Kearney Airbase in the Water Department, and then later on he worked at the Buffalo County Fairgrounds.

After a long and modest life, full of music and colorful conversation, he died at 94 years old. I always thought he died because he lost his hearing and could no longer visit, or he'd be alive today.

Anna Eliza (Piper) Thomas. About my mother. What can I say but she was the most wonderful person you would want to meet. She was born in Boone, Iowa in 1886. They moved to Gibbon, Nebraska when Mom was in her early teens. Her father farmed, and he passed on in 1925, the year I was born. Her mother was a dressmaker.

Mom went to rural school that only went to the eighth grade. But she kept taking the eighth grade over and over until she was in her late teens. Her love was twofold: she loved to crochet, and she could not put down a crossword puzzle until she had solved every word. I used her as my dictionary. I remember I ran across the word "pregnant" and asked what it meant. She was very embarrassed and stammered for a while to come up with the definition. In the seventh grade, I had a terrible time spelling "geography." Mom came up with a sentence to help me remember. She said take the first letter of each word of the full sentence and you will spell geography. It went: "George Elliot's old grandmother rode a pig home yesterday." I used that sentence for many years to spell geography.

Mom also loved to collect things. She and Dad would go to auctions, and if there was a salt and pepper set, they would buy it. I still have that collection of over 600 sets. She also collected dolls. She would make the clothes for them. My daughter, Lynda, was the only grandchild she would allow to hold any of them. Lynda has that collection. Mom was quite heavy and had arthritis. She wasn't the talker my dad was, but she loved to watch people. Mom also loved to flower garden. I can still see her standing among her bearded iris and white lilies, as she bends at the waist to pull a weed. Because of her arthritis, she could no longer bend at the knees, but she still minded her flowers.

Edith and Margaret Show. My sister Edith and her friend Margaret had a show called *The Edith and Margaret Show* on KGFW radio, and they sang once a week. Back then in the early thirties KGFW was in a little building-like garage located just across the street to the east of the present east entrance to Foster field. I remember KGFW as being in a little wood garage there. Strangely enough, at that time Margaret Hartman actually lived at 1902 Avenue D—this is the very home I bought in the early sixties for 3000 dollars for my growing family.

Dave and I sang there once. My brother Dave and I sang at the KGFW radio station once. I was about seven or eight years old. Dave played the guitar and was supposed to play as backup to my singing. I was supposed to sing "Jim," an old cowboy song. But when I got to the radio station and they put me in front of the microphone, I froze up and couldn't sing. So Dave had to play the guitar and sing.

Barn dance at the Armory. My brother Roy used to sing at what we called the Barn Dance at the National Guard Armory on south Central Avenue. The guy who acted as M.C. of the barn dance called himself Georgie Spicklemeyer and worked at KGFW.

Belly Rub Dance Hall. Dad used to play the fiddle at *The Belly Rub* dancehall. It was just north of the Amory and the Buffalo County Court House. The dancehall used to be *Dady's*, a busy hamburger joint. At *Dady's* I could buy ten hamburgers for a dollar. Bert Dady used to own it. He retired and rented it to a dance hall, and they got to calling it *The Belly Rub*.

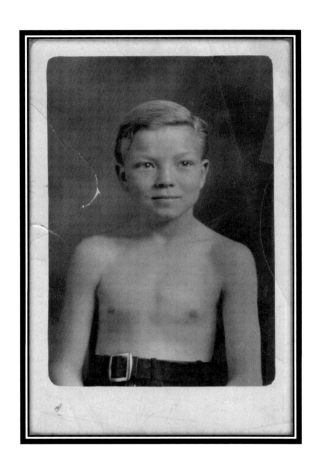

More Surgery

1935, more surgery. In 1935 I was sent to the orthopedic hospital in Lincoln again. This time they wanted to do surgery on me. They were going to try and graft a muscle they thought was good from one side of my leg, cut it in half, and then bring it up and attach it to my knee. And in the process to keep everything stable, a silver spike was driven through my leg just below my knee bone. And they drove another spike up the bottom of my foot into the bone.

In a letter to my mother from the hospital I wrote, "Please come down and get me. I have to have an operation if you don't. It would be just the same if I had the operation. So please come down and get me."

This heartfelt letter actually whispers of some shocking awareness of the times: since my family relied on the welfare system for my medical needs, the state did not have to get consent from my parents for surgery. To put it quite bluntly, the surgeons could just "cut and paste" at their own unlimited discretion.

This hospital stay lasted all summer of 1935, but Dad, Mother and my brother Art managed to come and visit me once. I must admit that I didn't like seeing them, though, because seeing them made it all the harder when I couldn't go home with them.

They drove down to Lincoln in a Model T Ford. The car broke down, and they parked it across the street from the hospital for a couple days. Dad went to the junkyard to find parts, and he fixed the car right there on the street. That's just the way you did things in those days.

Me in my summer clothes

My brother Art, sister Edith, & me with cats.

13

County drivers. We didn't have any money, so welfare always took me to the State Orthopedic Hospital in Lincoln. The county welfare had two drivers, one was Vern Freeman and the other was Bill Sweitzer. These two drivers would come around about four o'clock in the morning and pick up kids all over the area to go to what they called "observation day" in Lincoln. They always came on a Friday. And with two carloads full, we would start on our trip to Lincoln. Most the time getting there would take about five hours, so we would get there about nine o'clock in the morning. Each child would go in and see the doctor, and then they decided the treatment for me and the other children.

I don't remember what all happened the summer of 1936, but I know I went in the hospital for surgery that summer.

Running away from hospital. Then in 1937 when I was 12 years old, the driver picked me up in the early morning hours and took me to Lincoln for observation day. That Friday I was not expecting to stay there. I was expecting to go home. But after I got there, the doctors said they wanted to do surgery and keep me for the summer. And so the drivers went back to Kearney and left me in Lincoln.

I was heartbroken. I did not want to have any more surgeries! I did not want to be away from home all summer! But I had no choice because the welfare division had total control over me since my parents were poor and didn't have the money to make choices about my care. And there was no legal action you could do at the time anyway, even if you wanted to.

So I remember the Sunday after the Friday they left me there. I manufactured an idea to get back home. I knew I was a few miles south of Highway 6, and I knew Highway 6 was the way toward home. So that Sunday morning, I quietly ate my breakfast. Then I left the hospital and walked with the help of crutches across the street to the corner drug store. I hung around there for a little while, making sure no one followed me from the hospital or anything.

In this letter from the hospital to my mother, I write: "Please come down Saturday because I have to have a operation if you don't…"

Along with crutches at this time, I had a built up shoe and a ring caliber brace on my right leg. My right leg was weak and atrophied. Over time it became a several inches shorter than my left leg, so I needed the built up shoe to compensate for the difference in my two legs. The brace shop in Lincoln constructed the build up on the shoe out of cork and wrapped it in black leather to match the shoe. For years afterward I traveled to that Lincoln brace shop any time I got a new pair of shoes. Fortunately, my left leg had gotten some strength back, so I could put more of my weight on it.

After hanging out for a while and pretending to shop for a comic book, I left the drug store. I took off to the north until I came to O Street, and then I took O Street west to get out on Highway 6. I walked west on Highway 6 and across the bridge, which took me over the railroad tracks. That stretch was about a two-mile hike with crutches, brace, built up shoe—and just a reasonable assumption of how to get home.

Once I'd gotten across the bridge, I started putting my thumb out, hitchhiking west. I'd never hitchhiked in my life, but I'd seen other people do it. You just stand out next to the road and put your thumb out in a going-that-way pose. A car went by with a number nine county license plate on it and my heart just sank. My home was in nine county! Each county in the state had a number, and car license plates carried that number. And incidentally, nine county, my home county, is named Buffalo County.

There was my chance to get home. That Buffalo County car was long gone. So I started sticking my thumb out again to passing cars.

Pretty soon a car going east stopped, and the driver yelled, "Lynn, do you want a ride?"

That nine county car had turned around and come back for me. I got in, and he wheeled the car around and headed west. The driver turned out to be my own hometown family doctor, Dr. Edwards, and his wife and their two sons. They had been to the University of Nebraska football game the day before, stayed overnight in Lincoln, and were returning back to Kearney. They took me home. Afterwards, I learned that Dr. Edwards told my dad that he knew I was running away, but he did not have the heart to take me back to the hospital.

Our house was on Avenue I and about the end of 23rd street, right in there. It was a little four-room house with an outside toilet. I had Dr. Edwards drop me off on Highway 30, which was about a block and a half away from our house to the south. I climbed out of the car and walked across the field, which was just a plain grassy field back then but it is now built up with businesses. Our house is long gone.

As I walked across the field, I saw my dad come out of the house and go into the outside toilet. I walked up to the toilet, banged on the door and hollered through the door, "Hiya, Dad!"

And my dad pulled open the door, and there he stood, with a most surprised but happy look on his face, still adjusting his overalls from the interruption. Mother and Dad were both surprised, I'm sure, but here I was, back home again. My folks got a hold of the hospital down in Lincoln and told them I had gotten home. The hospital knew I'd run away, and they had the cops out looking for me in Lincoln. The doctors let me stay at home for about two weeks.

My main complaint at the time, I guess, was that I did not want to have surgery, and I didn't want to have to breathe in ether because it made me sick. Although ether had a number of side effects, including nausea, it was the most commonly used inhalation anesthetic at the time. So the doctors said they would do some tests and see if I was a candidate for a spinal anesthetic, which would deaden me from my waist down. This was a relatively new procedure in the summer 1937.

Also, I felt better since my mother got to ride down with me, and she stayed at a rooming house just down the street from the hospital. She got to stay with me until after my surgery. I had so many different surgeries, and I don't know which one this was, but I do remember staying in the hospital for the whole summer of 1937.

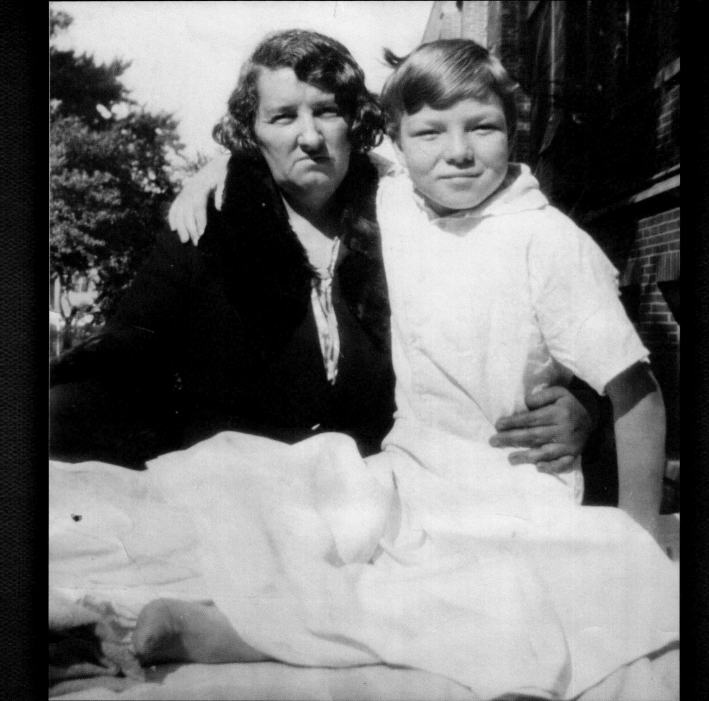

"I always remember those days as they were so lonely, but I made a lot of friends in the hospital."

Mom & Me at the hospital in Lincoln

Friends in the hospital.

Freddy Smith. They called him Freddy Smith but no one really knew his name. The story was that the hospital found him as a baby on their doorstep, and they took him in and cared for him all those years. They raised him at the hospital all his life. He was 20-some years old when I was there. Freddy's body was stiff as an oak board. Every joint bent at a 90-degree angle and every joint was just frozen. His hip angles were bent, his knees, his ankles, his wrists, elbows, every joint bent and frozen. Even his shoulders were frozen, keeping his arms stiff at his sides. Freddy's build and features were long and lean, adding to the somewhat peculiar visuals of frozen angles.

But Freddy didn't let that stop him from getting around. He'd lift up the foot flippers on his wheelchair, and then off he'd go, shuffling along as fast as he could down the hallways. Then he'd just use his feet for brakes. The hospital had inclines all over and he'd go down those and get around everywhere. Down in one area there was a pool table, and he'd go down there and shoot pool. He was amazing, with arms stiff and unyielding, he could shoot pool with the best of the guys. I heard years later that they found a way of straightening out his frozen joints, and that he became an architect at the state capitol. But I don't know if that's true.

Blondle Coon. Another friend at the hospital was Blondle Coon. Physically, he couldn't sit up in a wheelchair, so he used a wheeled hospital stretcher. The stretcher had big wheels on the front and little toggle wheels in the back. He lay on his stomach with his hands dangling over the end. He'd propel himself around by reaching down and moving the large front wheels on the front end of the stretcher. He rolled himself all over the place and came around and socialized with the rest of the guys.

Willie Wolf. Another one I remember was Willie Wolf, an Indian boy from the Winnebago Reservation, I believe. I think he had osteomyelitis, an infection of the bone or bone marrow. But I don't remember too much more about him.

Another Thomas. Plenty of strange things happened at the hospital. One strange thing happened to another kid with the same last name—Thomas. He had something wrong with his arm, polio I guess or some other problem with his arm, and he was having surgery the same day I was having surgery. His name was John Thomas and mine was Walter

Thomas. Well I came out of surgery with a leg cast on my right leg. And John Thomas came out of surgery with not only a cast on his arm, but also a cast on his right leg!

For a couple weeks we kept asking him, "John, what's wrong with your leg? Why do you have a cast on your leg?"

"I don't know," John said. "I didn't think there was anything wrong with my leg."

There wasn't anything wrong with his leg!   His mother was there at the time, and she couldn't figure it out either. She started asking a lot of questions. They finally got to investigating, and I guess they got confused in the operating room where they were putting casts on, and they not only put a cast on me, but then here's another Thomas and they put a cast on his leg too. Well, they had made a mistake, and they took that cast off his leg and sent him home pretty quick.

Bananas, Newspapers & Bicycle Dreams

Bananas, Newspapers & Bicycle Dreams

Coal and Art: My younger brother, Art, and I were very close and protected each other. When I was about nine and Art was about seven years old, we used to hang around the railroad tracks. In those days the coal was hauled by rail from the east to the west.   And sometimes the vibration would shake off a chunk of coal. So we would walk the tracks, dragging a burlap sack, looking for pieces of coal to burn in the furnace at home. At that time we lived at 1822 Avenue F, right on the corner, just a couple blocks south of the railroad tracks.

Trains at that time usually had two brakemen on the caboose and of course the engineer and fireman at the front. When they'd stop, one brakeman would walk on one side of the train and the other one would walk on the other side of the train, and they would check the wheels and all that, looking to see that everything was okay on the train cars. The brakemen would see us looking for coal along the tracks, and sometimes a brakeman would get up on the coal cars and knock off some coal for us.

Sometimes if there wasn't any coal on the ground, Art would climb up on one of the cars sitting there and throw some down. That coal would be in big chunks instead of the little ground up pieces we'd find on the ground.   Once in a while dad would get a ton of coal and have it put in the hole under the house where we had the furnace. The hole didn't go all the way across under the house. It was just a place to have the furnace and coal. I think it was five dollars for a ton of coal at that time. We didn't have much.

Dad was only making nine dollars a week at the time. But it was probably better than WPA in those days. Workers Progress Administration (WPA) was a federal program that Roosevelt used that kept people working. People working in the WPA built Harmon Park and garden and built the Armory. Later on, I think WPA workers got paid 50 dollars a month. Dad eventually did get a raise up to 19 dollars a week. During the war he got a job with the water department at the airbase for 50 dollars a week!

Art & me

22

Originally, the ground at the airport was all prime farm ground. The city had a little dirt airstrip on the east side for small planes. However, the federal government wanted that farmland for military uses, so they condemned the land and pressured people to sell for 50 dollars an acre. Colonel Arbuckle, a distant relative of my dad's, had a farm out on what is now 56th street at the north end of the desired properties. He held out and got 75 dollars an acre for his ground. He was the last one to sell. The government would buy it from you at a good price, but they really pressured you to sell. Then they built an airstrip, barracks and other buildings there on that good land.

During World War II, mostly the soldiers just came in to Kearney and gathered to make up a crew. Then they loaded up on a B-17 or a B-29 and went east and overseas. The soldiers came from all over the United States. On occasion there were 50,000 soldiers here at one time. They'd take over the whole area when they came to town. The military also used the Kearney location for other purposes such as working on military vehicles and such.

One man's junk Art and I used to walk all the way out to the airbase. Each of us pulled a gunnysack, and we picked up pop bottles and other things we could sell. We walked out on one side of the road and then back on the other side of the road. That's four miles out and four miles back. And we walked the alleys. I had a wood wagon tied to my crutch and pulled it along. We picked up pieces of iron or brass or anything we could sell to the junk yards. Martin Johnson ran the junkyard that sat where the city parking lot is now just east of what is presently the Chicken Coop Keno Parlor. Just around the corner to the south was Lederman's Junkyard, now the police impound lot on Avenue B and Railroad Street. Jack Lederman took it over from his dad.

Art and I weren't always all business looking for ways to make money or gather coal. Other times, just for fun, Art and I used to go to the button factory where they used seashells to make buttons. We'd dig around outside and find whole seashells, and then we could pretend it was our own day at the beach.

A fun benefit of living near the railroad tracks is that we were close by when the circus came to town. Nearly every year the circus would pull into town by rail and set up south of the tracks. Anderson Wrecking is located on that property today. Back in my childhood, those fields were filled with tents and animals and performers of a marvelous circus. Art and I would sit down at Kearney Livestock and watch the circus unload off the train cars. The elephants would pull the wagons that had the wild animals in them. They also used the elephants to help set up the tents, pulling ropes and wood beams.

Another fun memory is that we always remembered when it was Thursday. Every Thursday our neighbor, Mrs. Edna Courtier, made big, sticky wonderful cinnamon rolls! On that day all the kids in the neighborhood would drop their bikes, their dolls, their marbles—they dropped everything and beat a path to the Courtier house. A block away we could catch the aromas of hot bread and warm cinnamon, so even if you did forget it was Thursday, the delicious aromas wafting through the neighborhood would remind you.

Many years later I saw Mrs. Courtier and we shared wonderful reminisces of those wonderful summers of a simpler day. Mrs. Courtier did have a confession to make.

She said, "You know, when you used to play in our yard, I'd see you playing, and I'd wonder, how that poor little crippled boy is going to make it in life?"

Bubby. When I was little, my brother Merle had a hard time saying, "brother", so he called me "bubba", which became Bubby. The name stuck as a moniker of endearment, so the whole family always called me Bubby. To this day my family, extended family, and close family friends will still call me Bubby sometimes.

Short pants. Every couple years my Aunt Agnes would come to visit from Yuma, Colorado. On her visits, she'd help Mom with household chores like cleaning and laundry. On one visit Aunt Agnes was ironing clothes, and she became frustrated as she tried to iron my pants. As hard as she tried, she just could not get the pant legs to iron out the same length.

My mother laughed and said, "You won't get Bubby's pant legs to be the same length. I shorten one leg on his pants because one leg is shorter than the other, and he has a built up shoe."

Then as I grew, my pants were handed down to my younger brother Art. He didn't have one short leg, but he looked like he did because his pants were uneven!

Newspapers. It was very trying times. But all my life, everyone was good to me, including my first customers! When I came home from the hospital after 1937, I started peddling newspapers. Mostly I sold the *Saturday Evening Post*, *Ladies Home Journal*, and the *Pennsylvania Grit*.

My best running area was downtown from Avenue A to Central Avenue. On 21st Street just east of Central Avenue was a great little area. On the north side of the street was the *Arabian Nights* beer parlor managed by Joe Brock, and across the alley was John Higgins' pool hall. Across the street on the south side was George Tracy's beer parlor. I also sold at houses, but my favorite places were the beer parlors.

I would go into the smoky room, walk up to the first person I saw and ask, "Would you like to buy a newspaper?"

They'd say, "Yea, sure, I'll buy one from ya."

They gave me a nickel, and then they usually let me keep the paper! I might sell the same paper three or four times.

Selling *The Pennsylvania Grit*, I won a box camera, the *Number Two Hawkeye Junior* box camera. We took all our family pictures in the thirties with that camera. We took most of the old photos in this book with that camera.

Cloverine Salve. I also sold *Cloverine Salve*. This salve was good for just about everything, burns, whatever. I'd just go around to houses and sell. The Cloverine Company gave me colorful, eight-by-ten pictures as a bonus. But I also made a profit selling the salve. It wasn't as profitable as the newspaper, though, because people would buy the salve and keep it. They still make this product, and I have a tin of it sitting on my bathroom counter.

Another successful selling adventure involved candy bars and auctions. On Saturday afternoons in the summer, Walt Brown had auctions downtown in an empty lot a block north of what is now the Law Enforcement Center. I bought candy bars like Snickers and Milky Way at Kaufmann and Wernert's dime store. At the time you could buy one candy bar for a nickel or three candy bars for a dime. I'd buy three candy bars for a dime and take them over to the crowd at the auction and sell them for a nickel, giving me a nickel profit for every three bars sold.

Photo of me on the porch about the time I was selling newspapers in Tracy's bar downtown. Tracy's is now Copperfields, but the Tracy name is still on the building.

Punch board. One of my selling ideas was not exactly "above board." In this selling scheme of mine, I decided to buy a punchboard at the dime store for a nickel, and I bought a spoon for 15 cents.   The punchboard had a question behind each paper punch out. The spoon would be the prize if someone picked the punch with the right question behind it. The first place I went was the bar, and George Tracy paid me a dollar to punch them all out. Of course to my discomfiture, there was no question on there like the one I asked. The question I'd made up to win the spoon was of course not on the board.   The punch card had 100 punches, which I sold for a penny apiece, so I still made 80 cents. That was the first and only time I did that!

Eggnog & pocket full of eggshells. When we lived on Avenue I and 23rd Street, across the street from us lived the Evans, and they had a milk cow. They used to sell the cream, and I could buy the skim milk for a nickel a half gallon.

I took an empty half-gallon syrup can and walked across the street and they filled it with a half gallon of milk. I came home and broke two or three eggs into the half gallon of milk, added a tablespoon of vanilla, and then shook it up. That'd be my eggnog. To this day, I love eggnog.

During the school year at Emerson, I walked home for noon dinner. Before heading back to school, I gathered eggs from the hen house, and I put them in my overall pockets. One time I forgot to take them out of my pockets. When I got to school I discovered to my chagrin that I'd broken all the eggs in my pockets, leaving me with crunchy, yellow pockets of goo.

Christmas. I remember this one Christmas, I hung up my stocking, and I got a plastic comb and an orange. Another Christmas, I suppose I was eight or nine years old, and I got a little hand drill. I guess it probably costs the folks maybe 20 or 30 cents, but that was a lot of money to take 20 or 30 cents and buy extras. Life went on. I grew up.

Electric train, ABC Drug. There are so many great people I came in contact with while I was growing up. I remember in 1937, Mr. Walter Artman had a drug store called ABC Drug, and it was on the corner of Central Avenue and 23rd. I always liked the young clerks who worked there, as they smelled of Juicy Fruit gum and always had time and a friendly word for me.

The drug store had a contest to stimulate sales whereby customers could vote for kids to win an electric Streamliner Train. The lucky kid who got the most votes would win the train! I don't know exactly how it worked, how many points you got for how much you spent, but I know a lot of times people would come in and make purchases and not use their points.

"Do you want to vote for someone to win the train?" The clerk asked.

Sometimes the customer said, "Well, I don't know any of those kids."

And the clerk usually responded, "You could vote for Walter. He's a good kid."

Many of the customers voted for me, and I won the electric train! It was kind of a setup deal because the clerks all rooted for me to win it.

That was one of the many things that went on in my life—so many wonderful, wonderful people. And winning that fancy little train was quite a big deal at my house. My dad and my brother-in-law, Jerry Cure put the train together, and they became so enthralled with running the train, it was hours before me and my brother Art got to play with it.

Haircuts. Mike Hollinger's barbershop was downtown west of the beer parlors where I sold newspapers. I always remember Mike, as he was so kind.

When my hair would get too long, Mike would step out of the shop in my path and say, "Alright Tommy, it's time to cut your hair."

(He always called me Tommy as a nickname for my last name of Thomas.) He brought me in and set me down in his chair and cut my hair. He never charged me anything. He did that for a couple years there while that area was my stomping grounds.

Bicycle dreams. I dreamed that I would be able to ride a bicycle. Even though I couldn't push down with my right leg, I could push down with my left leg, so I dreamed I could get a bicycle without brakes on it and then the pedals could keep turning around. Then I would only have to push down on one side, and I could make it go.

On the corner downtown where I sold newspapers was a tire and battery shop called Yancey's, and Mr. Yancey had the shop there. Copy Cat Printing is there now. I went to Mr. Yancey, and I told him of my dream to ride a bike. He listened intently to my need for a bike with no brakes. Then he ordered a bicycle to my design without brakes on it, so the wheels would continuously go around. Also he agreed to a payment plan whereby I was to pay him a dollar something a week. And I did make all those payments, but I don't know exactly how long it took me to pay for it. I'm not sure what other bicycles sold for at that time, but I believe my bicycle cost about 15 dollars or so—with Mr. Yancey's discount of course.

In the end, though, my shiny red bike went to my younger brother Art to ride, for try as I might, I could not manage to ride the bike. My right leg was just too weak and cumbersome to assist the process of riding at all. Years later, though, my legs and I managed to handle successfully a car with a stick shift and clutch, a challenge for some drivers with two good legs.

Ed Verbeck, wooden leg. Ed Verbeck had the gas station over on 22rd and B on the southeast corner, and he liked to whittle wood on those slow afternoons. Ed had a wooden leg, but he got around as well as anyone with his wooden leg (and no, he didn't whittle his own leg). To Ed's chagrin, a Mrs. Keppie used to come by and talk and talk and talk to him. Since Ed needed to keep the station open, he was trapped like a caged cat, forced to listen to hours of endless chatter. Mrs. Keppie was a nice woman, but Ed just wasn't the visiting type.

Ed just couldn't take her talking any longer, so finally, Ed had an idea to make an end to all that talking. He whittled up a big penis and painted it for some extra realism. The next time Ed saw Mrs. Keppie walking up the driveway to stop by for an afternoon of chatter, he laid his "sculpture" in his lap, tucking it in the pant folds for a little extra credibility. Mrs. Keppie saw it, and shocked; she rushed out of the station and never came by to just talk again.

Nebraska River Hippo. I would go over to Ed's station and hang around, and sometimes he would take me with him down to the bar. People would buy him beers, and I'd sit and eat pretzels. Other times, we'd go fishing for catfish and carp down at the canal by the south Avenue M bridge. The tailrace starts up north by the college and then meanders through town like a snake. I used to fish all along the southern most section of the stream, both east and west of the Avenue M

29

Bridge. On current maps that part of the canal is labeled the North Channel Platte River, which pours into the Platte River.

One summer afternoon I sat quietly fishing on the canal bank, and a water moccasin came out of nowhere and slithered across my foot. There used to be several slaughterhouses along that part of the river, and lots of times I'd be sitting there fishing and a cow belly would come floating by. I imagined the expanded bellies as some species of Nebraska river hippo, lazily floating belly up down the Nebraska Nile. The slaughterhouses would just dump the cow innards right into the tailrace. But the catfish loved all that easy food.

Groceries. Saturday night was the big night in Kearney, and my folks would park on Central Avenue and watch the people. The favorite parking was on Central just north of 21st Street. (Nelson's furniture now occupies that section of downtown). In that area was located ABC Drug Store and O.P. Skaggs Grocery Store. We would do our weekly shopping on Saturday night. Dad and Mom would get five or six large paper bags full of groceries for five dollars. Dad was making about ten dollars a week at the time.

Kearney used to have grocery stores all over town; there seemed to be some kind of store in every neighborhood. Out on East 25th Street there was Jones Grocery where Bob's Super Store is now. On the other corner to the west was Acee Lund's filling station. A small neighborhood grocery could pop up anywhere because people would just turn their living room into a store. I remember Whitney's Store in their house over by Emerson School. Mrs. Lloyd had a grocery over on 18th Street and Avenue F, run by Emmett Brundige that we used for years while we lived in that neighborhood.

In the summer there was a local produce market or farmer's market if you will, downtown on the alley across the street from Tracy's beer parlor. The Carl Deebs family opened up that market every year. They had three boys: Tony was the oldest, Woodrow the youngest, and sadly, the middle son was killed in a plane crash in Italy during WWII. The whole family helped run the market. Inside and outside were woodbins and tables filled with all sorts of fresh vegetables and fruits. In the south part of Kearney, other families like Gabrells, Shada, and Georges raised small plots of vegetables for a living.

Schools & Teachers. I went through the Kearney Public School system, attending Bryant, Emerson, and Longfellow. Let me tell you about some teachers of my past in Kearney. There was Miss Long, first grade teacher at Bryant. She was also the principal of the school, while teaching 35 or more students. Miss Lavington, third grade teacher at Bryant, 34 students. Mr. Raymond Dimetz (Mr. D), sixth grade teacher at Emerson; he was also the Principal of Emerson, while teaching 35 students. His pay? Seven hundred dollars a year. I remember we had a little workshop in the basement of the school. Mr. D taught me how to make an alabaster powder box for my mother. Then there was Miss Nellis (wife of Harold Smith, M.D.) She taught eighth grade English. Miss Kibler, ninth grade English. At Junior High: Miss Shirley, Citizenship; Milton Beckman, Algebra. And then at Longfellow High School: Alice Parson, English Literature; Harvey Cole, Biology; Chester Marshal, Typing.

And then there was Richard (Dick) Dyer (he was my favorite), seventh grade Geography. He had a way about him like a philosopher that made you think, and a kinder, gentler person you would ever want to meet.   He came back after the Second World War and became a lawyer (my favorite lawyer).   Dick went from here to be a Federal District Judge.

In grade school we learned penmanship and how to add and subtract and multiply in our heads (no calculators). I'm not saying everything was taught necessarily in the best manner, but we all learned. These schools were two story buildings with a basement, and large windows that let the air circulate when it was hot. We never got out of school because it was too hot. There were no elevators, no single story schools.

And how I remember Mr. Forney, the janitor at Emerson: he stocked the furnace to keep us warm; he dusted the rooms and halls, swept the floors and rang the bell to call us into class after recess or to start school. Sometimes he allowed us to ring it for him. His son, Samuel Forney Sr. later became the head janitor and maintenance man of all the public schools.

Junior High. When I transferred from sixth grade to Junior High, I transferred my name as well. I started going by my middle name, Lynn, instead of using Walter for my first name. It is said that my sister Dorothy had a pretty good boyfriend named Walter at the time I was born, so I guess everyone thought that was a pretty good name. And I liked the name Walter, but a family friend named Walter drank too much, and I did not want to be like that. So I changed to using Lynn for my first name.

I made up a song in ninth grade right after the Japanese attacked Pearl Harbor. It went something like this:

More Men Like MacArthur

We need more men like MacArthur
As you very well know
His fame will grow,
From friend and foe
'Cause he's got the Japs by the toe, in Tokyo
Wherever you may wonder
On land or sea
He will bring America to Victory!

When I got into Junior High School, I was active with the rest of them, and I had perfect balance at that time. With my crutches swinging like dual pogo sticks, I could go up and down stairs like a shot. And a lot of times I would jump down like greased lightning, taking three steps at a time, and still be able to balance. I broke several crutches doing it, but I never got hurt coming down stairs.

Lynn Thomas
October 8, 1942

English 5
Period I

An Autobiography

The thing that stands out most in my mind was when I was about five years old. I came home from school one noon and felt sick. My head was heavy and I always wanted to sit down and rest my legs which felt very tired. Then one morning when I got up I couldn't walk. My felt gave way under me and I could hardly move. I was put back to bed and the doctor was called. No doctors knew what was wrong with me. I never could walk again by myself from that day on.

I still remember the days when I would look out the window at all the other kids playing and wish that I could go out there with them and play, but I couldn't.

Not one long year I lay in bed, then a great thing happened, I fell out of bed, and to get myself back upon it I tried to push myself back up on the bed. One of them worked and I got up by myself. From then on one leg got better and not long after my legs. And I was able to walk a little on crutches, and I think to this day I would be still laying in bed not able to move if I hadn't wanted to get out and play like other kids.

Then one day I was taken to the orthapedic hospital where I learned to swim and wood splints for over a year. They were very nice to me & I had all I could eat and went to a little play house in the afternoon. When I walked in a cast them after covered me from my toes to my chest and let to go home.

But in a few weeks I was back again for another operation. Then when I was twelve I had to go back again for another operation but this time I was old enough to know that I did not like being in a hospital alone. Been in the hospitals a few weeks. After I had started out it was about seven o'clock in the morning, I started itching for some

Bananas. At this time we were living in an old two-story house on Railroad Street and Avenue F. It sat on a wedge of property that is now under the Avenue H overpass onramp.   The house was drafty and creaked like an old bed frame everywhere, but it was close to where my dad worked over at the Kearney Livestock, straight south of us across the railroad tracks.

I walked home from junior high, and I walked past the wholesale fruit house on Railroad Street, where they sold fruit and vegetables to the grocery stores. The wholesale house bought big stalks of bananas, and if the banana had even one little black spot, they took it off and tossed it into a wood barrel. There really wasn't anything wrong with them; they'd just have a ripe spot or little bruise. To my great luck, I found out about that barrel!

It got so every time I walked by the fruit house, one of the workers would yell over to me, "Hey kid, do you want some bananas?"

 I got a paper bag and they filled it full of bananas out of the barrel. These were lean times, so we ate a lot of bananas. If there weren't any bananas in the barrel, many times the guys there would take out a new stalk and take off the ones with a black spot. Then I'd have some bananas to take home with me. Everybody was so kind to me in those growing up years.

Dry, dusty, hot. Those were very tough times as it was not only during the depression of the thirties, but also it was during the seven-year drought of the dust bowl. I remember the dust got so bad that you could hardly breathe, and the dust settled everywhere in the house. We didn't have it as bad as the center of the dustbowl in southwest Kansas and the Oklahoma Panhandle, but we still had it bad enough. During those years the dust would blow in from all over the Great Plains, huge rolling clouds of black, red, grey, or yellow; the clouds would be the color of whatever area's sad topsoil was being carried away that day.

In my English class autobiography from 1942 I write, "The thing that stands out most in my mind was when I was about five years old, I came home from school one noon and felt sick . . ."

We lived at 1822 Avenue F at the height of the Dust Bowl. Mrs. Lloyd had her little grocery store on 18th Street and Avenue F, a block away, and a guy by the name Emmett Brundige ran the store for her. One windy, dust-filled day, my dad walked the block to Mrs. Lloyd's store, lost his billfold in the dust and never did find it.

It was sad and hard times for livestock owners. For the most part, there was nothing for animals to eat—no grass, no feed, nothing. It got so bad, the government offered to pay a dollar a head for cattle, calves and horses you couldn't feed. Then they dug a big hole west of Kearney Livestock. People brought in their starving animals, pathetic creatures with gaunt frames, barely more than walking shadows. We lived close by, and I watched as they led each animal up next to the hole. Then one by one, they shot them in the head and pushed them in the hole.

Then briefly—one single day in the middle of all this heat and drought and dust—the sky opened up, and it rained buckets and buckets full of big fat raindrops. The downpour dumped so much water so fast on the parched land that the Platte River flooded clear up to 11th Street, which is a couple or so miles from the riverbanks. This deluge seemed like some insane, cruel joke from Mother Nature.

Hot summers at the hospital. Nearly every hot summer of the thirties I spent some time, if not all summer, at the Orthopedic Hospital in Lincoln. At the hospital they didn't have air conditioning. They opened the windows, and I became instantly homesick as I heard all the sounds of life outside the hospital. Most nostalgic was the early morning clippity-clop of horses' hooves on pavement as the horses pulled milk delivery wagons on the street. Sometimes I heard the distant sound of a train whistle from a train going somewhere—maybe going toward home, I imagined.

When I got my first pigeons at about 13 years old, my dream was to have more pigeons than anyone in town, and that dream did come true. At the time we live on East 25th Street in a house that still sits just west of the present Northwestern Gas Company. Elmer Williams owned the house. I had an old chicken coup, but I had lots of pigeons. And as time went on, I had some fancy pigeons: some White Kings, Duchess, Red Carneaus, Tumblers, and Homing Pigeons. Roy Zimmerman had a modest pen of pigeons in a humble barn over on Avenue C, and I got some of my fancy pigeons from him. Mostly I had "commys," a.k.a. common pigeons.

Racing homers. Another way I added to my little flock is with eggs. Years ago some pigeon-racing enthusiasts shipped their racing homers to Kearney as a race starting point. Mostly the pigeons were from Chicago, and they took them up to Reservoir Hill for release. The field they used for release is now Memorial Field, where the pigeons probably watch baseball from the fences. Back then, I loved to be there to watch the release. When they released them, the birds would take off, and they'd circle and circle above us, then off they'd go, headed east toward their Chicago home. Sadly, hawks would grab a lot of pigeons on their perilous trip. The pigeons were shipped in crates by train, and sometimes there'd be eggs in those crates, and sometimes the man handling the release would let me take some of those eggs. Filled with the adrenalin of watching the release, I'd take them home and put them under my own pigeons, and then I'd have some beautiful racing homers! All these years later, by a strange coincidence I've had registered homing pigeons show up in my garage—twice. I made some calls and one owner came from North Platte to pick up his homer.

Pigeons, Lloyd Frank, and the great train robbery. One day while we were living on East Hwy 30, I went to the pen, and some of my birds were gone. I swallowed hard and my heart raced, as I knew they were stolen. So I went to see Lloyd Frank, who was Chief of Police at that time. I told him about my pigeons being stolen. I always remember that he listened to me. Here I am, maybe 13 years old, and he listened to me like it was a great train robbery. And he went to work and recovered my pigeons. Lloyd is a very nice man, and I never forgot him the rest of my life. When he ran for sheriff, he ran as a republican. My folks had been democrat all those years; however, when I got to be 21 one years old, and it happened Lloyd was running for sheriff on the Republican Party, I registered as a republican so I could vote for him for sheriff. He won and he was sheriff for a number of years. And we became very close friends in later years.

Chickens, pigs and Herefords. When I was 15 years old, somehow we got a loan through what they called Production Credit Association (PCA), a federal program that came out of the Farm Credit Act of 1933. The credit was extended so people could purchase farm equipment and livestock and operate farm related businesses. In our back yard we built a pen and a windbreak as part of a building. And I think we had four Hereford heifers in that pen.

We also bought a young female hog, and when the sow got older, she had piglets. There were several vacant lots around us with weeds growing on them. So when my brother Art and I came home from school at night, we would herd them all out to the vacant lots to eat the grass. After a couple years the sow started grabbing chickens to eat, and we just couldn't have that.

So I took the sow to a guy who fattened her up for me. He had a little coral down along the tailrace where he fattened a few pigs and steers. I told him about this sow that was eating chickens, and he said to bring her down and he'd fatten her up. Then I sold that sow for 80 dollars to buy my first car, a 1932 Chevy Coup.

Ring a chicken's neck. We also had chickens. Mother usually bought 50 or 100 chickens every spring. And so whenever company happened to come by, Mother said, "Bubby go ring a chicken's neck."

I would go catch one of the young roosters and ring its neck. And mom soaked it in hot water, pulled the feathers off, cut it up, and fried it.   After cooking the chicken, she put milk and flour in the skillet, and stirred it all up to make the best milk gravy you ever tasted. She also peeled some potatoes from the garden and cooked them. So we'd have fried chicken, potatoes and gravy for dinner, what we called the noontime meal. Food that fresh, made with such love has a unique, delicious dimension of flavor that I can recall to this day.

I learned to work early on as a youngster, and some of the responsibility of taking care of the chickens fell to me. One summer day, I spent the afternoon raking up and cleaning the chicken yard. My good friend Don Nelson watched and waited for me, so we could be off fishing. I finally finished, and I handed the rake to Don while I moved a bucket.

At that precise moment, my dad stepped outside, and seeing the clean pen, he said, "Good job, Don."

My friend Don Nelson and me.

He sent a postcard to me at the hospital. Notice the address is simply Lincoln Nebraska Orthopedic Hospital.

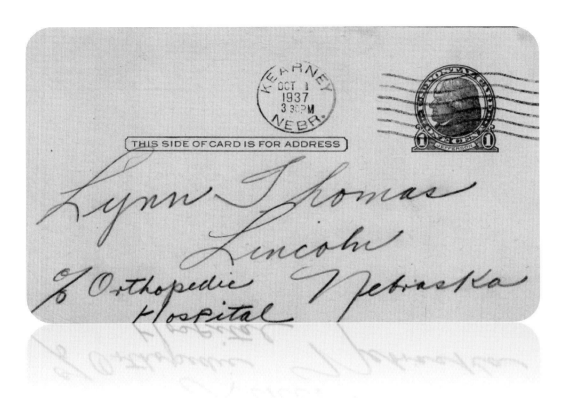

UNITED STATES OF AMERICA
OFFICE OF PRICE ADMINISTRATION

327835 AV

WAR RATION BOOK No. 3

Void if altered

NOT VALID WITHOUT STAMP

Identification of person to whom issued: PRINT IN FULL

(First name)   (Middle name)   (Last name)

Street number or rural route _____

City or post office _____   State _____

AGE	SEX	WEIGHT Lbs.	HEIGHT Ft. In.	OCCUPATION
17			5 Ft. 6 In.	

SIGNATURE
(Person to whom book is issued. If such person is unable to sign because of age or incapacity, another may sign in his behalf.)

WARNING
This book is the property of the United States Government. It is unlawful to sell it to any other person, or to use it or permit anyone else to use it, except to obtain rationed goods in accordance with regulations of the Office of Price Administration. Any person who finds a lost War Ration Book must return it to the War Price and Rationing Board which issued it. Persons who violate rationing regulations are subject to $10,000 fine or imprisonment, or both.

OPA Form No. R-130

LOCAL BOARD ACTION

Issued by _____
(Local board number)   (Date)

Street address _____

City _____   State _____

(Signature of issuing officer)

FOLD BACK

The Stamps contained in this Book are valid only after the lawful holder of this Book has signed the certificate below, and are void if detached contrary to the Regulations. (A father, mother, or guardian may sign the name of a person under 18.) In case of questions, difficulties, or complaints, consult your local Ration Board.

Certificate of Book Holder

I, *the undersigned*, do hereby certify that I have observed all the conditions and regulations governing the issuance of this War Ration Book; that the "Description of Book Holder" contained herein is correct; that an application for issuance of this book has been duly made by me or on my behalf; and that the statements contained in said application are true to the best of my knowledge and belief.

_____ [Book Holder's Own Name]
(Signature of, or on behalf of, Book Holder)

Any person signing on behalf of Book Holder must sign his or her own name below and indicate relationship to Book Holder _____ Son

_____
(Father, Mother, or Guardian)

OPA Form No. R-200

UNITED STATES OF AMERICA

War Ration Book One

WARNING

1 Punishments ranging as high as *Ten Years' Imprisonment or $10,000 Fine, or Both*, may be imposed under United States Statutes for violations thereof arising out of infractions of Rationing Orders and Regulations.

2 This book must not be transferred. It must be held and used only by or on behalf of the person to whom it has been issued, and anyone presenting it thereby represents to the Office of Price Administration, an agency of the United States Government, that it is being so held and so used. For any misuse of this book it may be taken from the holder by the Office of Price Administration.

3 In the event either of the departure from the United States of the person to whom this book is issued, or his or her death, the book must be surrendered in accordance with the Regulations.

4 Any person finding a lost book must deliver it promptly to the nearest Ration Board.

OFFICE OF PRICE ADMINISTRATION

Home at Fairgrounds. While I was in high school my mother inherited 400 dollars from her mother's estate. My folks used this money as the down payment on a house of their own. After renting and moving 13 times in the 17 years of my life, it was time for my family to have a little homestead of our own. This house still sits on the Buffalo County Fairgrounds and faces south just east of the Extension Building.

When we moved in the house was pretty lean on amenities. There was no electricity, no bathroom, no sewer, and no running water inside at the time. There was just the one gas lamp hanging from the ceiling inside, and out back we had an outhouse and a hand pump. We carried water from that pump to the house for household use as well as water for bathing. Later we built a wash shed out back of the house that we used to wash clothes. We had a wood stove out there to heat the water in a big tub for washing.

For two or three years Dad worked at the fairgrounds during the summer, and then during the rest of the year, he watched over the fairgrounds for no compensation. During the years working for the fairgrounds, Dad got city water piped in through the fairgrounds line, so we had indoor running water. Eventually we connected to the city sewer line as well. Bear in mind this was out in the country at that time. Corn and soybeans were raised across the road to the south, and an irrigation well sat on the corner.

Dad and I hauled wooden boxes from the junk pile at the airbase. We took them apart and used the lumber from them to build a two-car garage. We set the studding so the boards would just reach the upright 2x4's and could be nailed together. Back then, everyone reused what they could. Even Henry Ford had tire companies ship him his tires in a particular sized wood box so he could reuse that wood in truck beds. These were times when a person used everything.

A couple of my war ration books dated 1943

My folks gave 1100 dollars for this home, the first—and only—house they ever owned. They were 57 years old at the time. I was in high school by this time and Art just a couple years behind me. So this close to having an empty nest after 11 births, they get their own home to shelter them in their twilight years and to hold their extensive family for visits.

Later as adults, some of my siblings and I gathered with our families at the fairgrounds house, and there was always singing and music. We sang harmonies of the old songs and someone always had a guitar and a fiddle.   These were wonderful warm afternoons of musical energy.   Meanwhile, the young cousins raced in and out, playing tag and hide and seek at the weeping willow out front and eating pickles on the back porch.

Uncle Clayton and Fairgrounds house. Dad had a brother in Chicago, Uncle Clayton, and they had two daughters. Shortly after we moved into the fairgrounds house, they came out to Nebraska for a visit. We didn't have running water or anything, and those girls couldn't believe what hillbillies we were out here. We always just figured they were stuck up and snooty. Clayton hauled gasoline around to filling stations around Chicago. They paid more around Chicago, so they had more money than we did.

Out Back of the Fairgrounds House

High School friends: my brother Art, Chuck Kennedy, Me & Leroy Kennedy

HIGH SCHOOL

Highschool. When I was a junior in high school, I thought, I'm going to need to go to college and get an education. I hadn't taken school real seriously until then. So in the 11th grade I had to go back and pick up algebra. And as a senior I had to pick up biology and a couple other classes. I remember in the algebra class, I was an 11th grader and I had to go back with the ninth graders in junior high to take algebra. Milton Beckman was the algebra teacher.

We didn't print a yearbook for my graduating class of 1944. All extra resources were focused on the war, so the decision was made to not print the Kearney High School Log that year. I did get a copy of the 1943 Log. In one picture from the yearbook, I am dressed in coveralls and helping work on a car in auto mechanics class.

We didn't print a yearbook for my graduating class of 1944. All extra resources were being focused on the war, so the decision was made to not print The Kearney High School Log that year. I did get a copy of the 1943 log.

CAR EXPERTS — Robert Pfeil, Mark Binderup, Lynn Thomas receive practical experience in motor fundamentals.

Tiny Tone Radio. When I was in the 11th grade, I got a job at Tiny Tone Radio. Paul and Woody Beshore started the business. They built little crystal radios. At the time I worked for them, I tested crystals. The business was located in a building just north of city hall, facing east on Avenue A. On the ground level was a garage called Weismens. The Tiny tone Radio was on the second floor. One night there were four of us on duty working, including two other young guys, a jokester, by name of Charley Lamb, and then me. The three of us were trying to work, but Charley was clowning around and it was hard not to watch. He was standing up on a workbench, flapping his arms and crowing like a rooster. Just then, Don, one of the superintendents walked in on Charley's chicken dance with the rest of us watching. He fired us all on the spot.

Kearney Livestock. In the twelfth grade I got a job at Kearney Livestock. Farmers from the area brought their livestock to be sold through the Kearney Livestock. Mainly they brought in cattle, sheep, and pigs. Buyers came from all over to bid on the livestock. My job entailed sitting at the scales with Charley Riley. Charley was the scale master. In small groups the livestock were brought in from the pens in the back and locked in the little pen on the scale. Charley recorded their weight. Then the animals were herded into the sale ring, and the highest bidder bought the pen. Next they were herded out of the ring and sent to the pens in the back. It was my job to record the buyer's number and assign a pen number. Somehow I sent two different buyer's hogs to the same pen. This mixed up their hogs together, and there was no way to tell whose hog belonged to which buyer. Ray York fired me.

TinyTone Radio Co. was founded in 1935 in Kearney, Nebraska, by Paul Beshore and his brothers, making crystal receivers, based on a prefixed crystal diode patented by Paul Beshore in 1933. This pocket radio was about as big as a matchbox and was called TinyTone.

This advertisement from Popular Mechanics shows a Tiny-Tone crystal receiver made in 1936. The radios could be ordered by mail. They came in four different colors.

In the early 1940s the company changed its name to Western Manufacturing Co.

NEW!! MIDGET POCKET RADIO

$2.99 Complete Postpaid

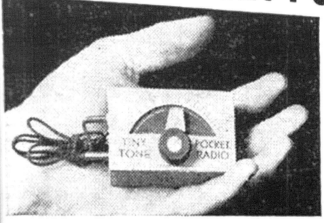

Fits in any small pocket easily. Weighs only 4 ozs. as shown. Comes in four beautiful colors; (Black, green, brown, white). NO tubes, batteries, or electrical connections needed! Nothing to wear or need replacement—will last for years—only one moving part! Separates and receives broadcast stations with beautiful clear tone. Range up to 50 miles—MUCH GREATER under good conditions—very little static or interference! Can be used by ANYONE ANYWHERE! NO CRYSTALS TO ADJUST! Absolutely complete with midget phone and instructions to use while in bed, hotels, autos, offices, camps, on bicycle or any place you may be. No complicated or messy hookups—takes only a second to connect! THOUSANDS OF SATISFIED OWNERS. THESE ARE FACTS. Send only $1.00 and pay postman $1.99 plus postage on arrival or send $2.99 (Cash, Money Order, Check). Ideal Gift. Guaranteed. ORDER NOW! (Foreign orders 65c extra.) (State color.)

TINYTONE RADIO CO., Dept. P-8, KEARNEY, NEBRASKA

COLLEGE

College. When I graduated from high school in 1944, the State of Nebraska offered me entrance in a rehabilitation program whereby the state helped me go to college in Lincoln at the University of Nebraska. The state paid some on tuition, books and lodging. I thought I would be an agriculture teacher, so I went to Ag College.

Blanche and Harry. I drove my 1932 Chevy Coupe to Lincoln. I went directly to State Capital where I met Mr. Armstrong, who was with the State Department of Rehabilitation. The state found a private home for me to live in while attending college. He drove north on R Street, and I followed him past the state fairgrounds, then on to Holdrege and to 42nd and Starr Street. There he introduced me to Blanche and Harry McNerney. Blanche is matronly, with hair in a bun; Harry is a little skinny guy. Both are really nice people. Their home is cozy and well kept. They rented me a second floor sleeping room, which had a bed, dresser and little desk. Blanche kept the room clean and washed the laundry. The state paid her 15 dollars a month for that room. The bathroom was down the hall, just around the corner. Harry & Blanche had a room across from me, and there were two other rooms at the end the hall. Their children had grown up and left home. Blanche rented out one of the extra rooms to a schoolteacher, and for a while, a foster child used the other room. Blanche's mother, Mrs. Pantier, a remarkably intelligent woman, lived on the first floor.

Harry owned a little one-man grocery store just north of their home. If there'd been an alley their house would have been across the alley at the back of the store.

Blanche was a wonderful influence on me. Blanche and Harry were religious and always wanted me to join the Baptist church. I went to the Baptist church with them a number of times, but I never joined the church. Blanche had a very beautiful record player with many records, mostly classical. There were two records that I most enjoyed. One was Nelson Eddy in *Tramp, Tramp, Tramp, Along the Highway.* The other was a Frank Sinatra record. On the main side was the song *Night and Day,* and on the other side was a tune that never caught on, but to me is the best, called, *Lamplighters Serenade*. I played that side over and over and used to sing that song constantly.

Many years later, Harry died and whenever I was in Lincoln I would take Blanche out to dinner, sometimes we'd go to a pancake house on O Street. During one of those dinners, we got to talking religion and creation—she never gave up trying to convert me.

I told her, "I have a difficult time believing that God created this earth from thought."

What she said next hit me like a ton of bricks. "Everything you see was created or started with thought," she said. "That chair, the street outside, this table—before it could be built, someone had to think of it."

Eating, Bluebird Cafe. Blanche was a great one about breakfast, and they charged me three dollars per month for my breakfast, which I was to prepare by myself. Since Harry had his own grocery store, there was always milk, breakfast food and bread to toast. That was my breakfast. Since money was scarce, this became my routine: I'd eat breakfast in the morning, no lunch, and then at night I'd go with my buddies down to the Bluebird Café for the hamburger steak dinner special. Price: 25 or 30 cents. The meal consisted of a salad, hamburger steak, potatoes, gravy, bread, butter, and a glass of milk. And that would cover me for the rest of the day. So usually I would just have the two meals: breakfast in the morning and the hamburger steak at the Bluebird Café. The state gave me about 20 dollars a month to help cover some expenses like food.

Friends. When I took my freshman entrance exams, I met Chris Christianson and Lou Ledyard from city campus. We became quick friends and shared many happy times while going to school. They lived at the YMCA.

Lou was from Elwood, Nebraska and studying to be a pharmacist. When Lou was a child he had a disease that caused the loss of his hearing in one ear, and he lost one eye. He had a glass eye and a hearing aid, so he was considered physically disabled. He was a good student in college. If the Y was noisy, he could shut off his hearing aid and concentrate in the midst of all kinds of ruckus. We went to the movies, and his glass eye got all watery. He was embarrassed about it, so we went in the bathroom and he took his eye out and washed it while I stood guard and held the door closed. Lou and I kept in some contact over the years, and he ended up living as a pharmacist in Kearney, Arizona.

My friend, Chris—real name Kenard—Christianson was from Holdrege. I don't know what happened to Chris after college; he started as Pre-med, but I think he flunked out of it when he got in trouble with one of the professors. The last I'd heard he was a radio announcer in Alaska.

Another friend, George Schmidt was at the Ag College. He came from Ralston Nebraska. He had polio too, but not as bad as I did. He could walk: just one leg bothered him. Not sure why, but George and I didn't immediately like each other, but then as time went on we became great friends.

The YMCA. The Y was located about the corner of 17th and P. Lou, Chris and I had some other friends there at the Y, and lots of us would do all kinds of things together besides eating dinner at the Bluebird Cafe. We played penny poker; we kept running books on the winnings and losses, and in the end, no one would end up owing anything. I learned to play chess there. Many winter nights and weekends, we played chess up in the rooms. Years later I taught my kids to play chess, and on long winter weekends we'd have family chess tournaments. My love of chess also turned into a love of the creative variety of chess sets, so I started collecting them. My first chess set was carved out of wood thread spools, and I still appreciate that set most. I've gone on to collect chess sets that range with themes from Star Wars to the Civil War to wine glasses—and everything in between.

My buddies and I loved to pull pranks or little high jinks on the unsuspecting. When Lou and I turned 21, a few of us went to a bar and had one beer. We dreamed up to call Chris and fool him and say that Lou was getting beat up. We made the call in a nearby phone booth, and then we quickly drove over and parked in front of the Y. Pretty soon the front door flies open and out runs Chris with a whole herd of guys racing and ready to go down there and help Lou. Sometimes we'd get on the bus, sit in different spots on the bus, and then we'd all quietly start yawning. It was hard to contain our laughter as we watched as the unsuspecting passengers would begin yawning one after another. One time we went to a high school football game and came back on the bus. There was about six of us and we formed a half circle outside the Walgreens on O Street. We put a hat on the sidewalk and started singing, pretending to sing for money.   I'm not sure if anyone ever tossed any money in the hat, but we sure had fun doing it.

I went to Ag College with Eldon Terrell and he was always up for some fun. He had a 1928 Pontiac four door sedan from some old people who had stored it for most of its life. The car was in mint condition. He put this whistle-like-siren on the exhaust, and you could pull a handle in the car and make it sound off. We came back to Kearney one weekend in his car, and we blew that whistle when driving past cattle and horses, and they'd take off running. Unfortunately, he blew it in town in Lincoln and got caught, and the cops made him take it off.

Pogo stick. Things didn't change in college and I stayed a daredevil on crutches. One day while headed to class in the educational building at the Ag Campus, I was going up the middle of this big wide stairway and my right crutch went out from under me. I watched as the crutch went sliding to the bottom of the stairs. Instead of going to the side and scooting down the stairs to retrieve my crutch, I got on my left crutch and bounced down to the bottom like a kid on a pogo stick.

Hair like wool. While going to the university Ag College, in Animal Husbandry class under Professor Alexander, we were studying different grades of wool from sheep. We evaluated the different grades. Some grades were coarse and stiff, but some grades were wonderful to the touch, smooth and silky; they were so soft.   When I came home that summer, I asked an attractive gal named Mary to go to the show with me. We went to the show and after the show we came home to sit on the porch swing. I touched her hair, and, thinking of the fine textured wool I'd felt at school, I said, "Your hair feels like wool." Oh, god, she got mad at me and stomped off. She never did speak to me again.

Cultivate corn. One summer break at home in Kearney, Charley Eckoff asked if I'd come work for him and help cultivate corn. They just lived down the street from us on the north side of 34th street by the railroad tracks. He had about 25 acres he farmed.

"Come on down, and I'll teach you how to drive a tractor," Charley said.

The problem is my left leg is so weak that I have to push it down with my hand to push the clutch in, so driving a tractor can be a daunting task. But I get on the tractor and drive around the yard a while. He hooks up the cultivator and rides back on it, operating the levers that run the hoes that cultivate the rows. I think I hear him yelling, and I look back to see Charley waving frantically as I'd been going over the corn not the rows. I did learn to cultivate, though, and I helped him with that little section, driving the tractor, in spite of having to push down on my leg to run the clutch.

Lifting my legs. Driving a clutch in a car, under snap decision driving conditions, could prove to be not only daunting but complicated! If driving a clutch, I had to use my hands to physically lift my left leg up and down to press the clutch, and I had to lift my right leg onto the gas and brake. My right foot also had a cumbersome built up shoe with about a five-inch solid wedge glued on the bottom. For some it is a simple process to drive and apply the brakes to stop the car. For me it is a multi step process:

1) with my left hand, lift my left leg up and put it on the clutch
2) push my left leg down on the clutch
3) kick it out of gear with my right hand (gear shift is on the floor)
4) grab the emergency brake and pull it back and lock it
5) reach down and pick up my right leg and put it on the brake
6) with my right hand push my right leg down on the brake
7) all the while, my hands are switching back and forth off and on the steering wheel.

Acknowledging that I needed extra time for maneuvering my car, I always drove defensively. Then one day Lou and I are driving down the street, and this guy pulls in front of me and—bang! I hit him in the rear end of his car. And I didn't just hit anyone. I hit General Guy Henninger, head of the National Guards.

Watching me fly though the steps to stop, Lou said, "God, I never saw somebody go through so many motions, so fast, to try and stop in my life!"

I didn't carry insurance in those days, not everyone did. The General said it was his fault, so we didn't have to do anything about it. He went his way and I went my way.

Later Lou kidded me and said, "Of all the people you have to hit, Lynn, you have to hit a general's car!" That was the first wreck I ever had, and I am fortunate in that my entire driving career has been a safe one.

Tires. I loved that little '32 Chevy Coupe, but we did have more problems at times. One weekend I headed home from Lincoln to Kearney with great intentions of a short weekend visit to my folks and friends. I drove from Lincoln to Seward on Highway 34 when suddenly a tire went flat. I pulled into this old filling station, and the guy put a patch on it called a "blow out patch." I now know why they called it a blow out patch: I got about three miles outside of Seward, and the tire went flat again. Because of World War II, tires had been rationed for a couple of years, and it was still nearly impossible to find even a used tire to buy. I had no alternative but to keep going, driving slowly along on the rim. At Aurora, though, the highway turned into bricks, and those bricks tore up the wheel. The further I drove, the more spokes came out. By the time I reached Grand Island, all the spokes were gone. I called Dad and he brought me a wheel and tire, and I drove home from there.

My second year in college, Dad found me a '34 Ford V8 with suicide doors. I rode to Kearney on the bus and drove the car back to Lincoln. This Ford was fast and fun, and actually had the reputation as a hot rod. Hot rod enthusiasts would strip off extra weight on the car and soup up the engines. And at the time it was the choice of bank robbers because the Ford V8 was the fastest car going. The rarer Ford coupe like mine had rear-hinged suicide doors and unique for having three windows—one on each door and the rear window.

When I sold the Chevy in Lincoln, a guy came over at night. I showed it to him under a streetlight, and he bought it for 150 dollars. Three years later I was out on the west end of Kearney at the Sinclair station when a little Chevy coupe drove in. It looked so much like my old car that I just had to get a closer look. And sure enough, it was my old car. I could tell for certain because the trunk had hinges on it that I'd installed to make it into a rumble seat. The couple driving the car said they bought it at a junk yard in Lincoln. They'd driven out to Kearney to visit a friend at the TB hospital.

1947 City Campus. One day it dawned on me that I can't even saw a board straight. I am not mechanically minded, so I just wouldn't be able to be an Ag teacher. So I transferred to city campus and I took up radio broadcasting, script writing, chemistry and history. It's now spring of 1947, and I'm in my second year of college.

Professor Morgan seemed to like my voice. We used to do little skits pretending like we were on the radio. We also wrote scripts for commercials and narratives for plays. The university had a radio program every weekend where they gave the university news. Professor Morgan matched me up with one of the senior girls to do the university news one week. As I recall the girl changed the typewritten script and wrote some handwritten notes to change the text of it. I couldn't read what she'd written and couldn't follow along, so I got confused and mixed up and I really screwed it up big time. So I didn't get asked anymore to be on the university radio show, and that was the end of my radiobroadcasting career. I certainly couldn't become a radio announcer since I almost flunked that course because of what happened on the radio incident.

Johnny Carson was going to school there at the same time, and we were both sophomores that year. I didn't know him, but we very easily could have passed each other in the halls of the communication department.

Above: College buddy Eldon Terrell & Me

Right: My '32 Chevy Coupe I bought when I sold my sow that started eating the chickens.

AFTER COLLEGE

Jobs. I only went to college for the two years down at the University of Nebraska in Lincoln. My folks just couldn't afford the gas money for my car, and the state ran out of money for my schooling. So I moved back home to my folk's house at the fairgrounds. I thought I'd get a job somewhere. But the wide variety of college classes I'd taken didn't really prepare me to work for any business in particular. By this time I drove a '33 Ford car that Dad gave me.

Figures don't lie, but liars figure. Then I decided some business experience could help in my job prospecting, so I signed up for a short summer course at the Kearney State Teachers College. As it turned out, I ended up in an accounting course with a young professor by name of Stretch Welch. I always remember the things he taught me about accounting and business and people. And these are things I lived by when I was entering the business field and working for people. I did learn accounting, but I wasn't able to utilize it until later on in the next two or three years.

Stretch had one lesson that he repeated every single day: "Remember this," he said, "figures don't lie, but liars figure."

And I'll always remember that proverb—in part because he said it so many times! Afterward, Stretch and I became really close friends, and it was a friendship that lasted until he died a couple years ago.

Insurance Office. I got a job as a secretary in an insurance and real estate office. Jim Cleary ran the insurance part of the business. Ed Neustrom ran the real estate part of the business. And between the two of them, they paid me 15 dollars a week. I would answer the phone, and I did some of the typing of the adjustments to some of the policies or something like that. But I was living at home at the time, so it didn't cost me much to live. Imagine earning 15 dollars per week! Why, I could go to the show for a quarter, get twelve hamburgers for a dollar. Gas was 20 cents a gallon (not many taxes in those days).

The bricks downtown. Their business office was right downtown in a rented space along the north side of the present day Kearney radio station building on 22nd Avenue. The building has long since been remodeled into a modern brick building, and there are only windows along that side of the structure. But years ago that was the Platte Valley State Bank building, and on the north side of building were small rental spaces for various businesses or interests. There were stairs leading up to each space on the upper level, and stairs leading down to the garden level spaces. Our office was upstairs. Medley's barbershop was on the garden level at the end next to Central Avenue.

The *Checker Club* was also on the garden level, and it was a popular place for years. Jud Henline paid the rent on the place; Jud is also the person who commissioned George Holmes to carve my first chess set. In some ways, the *Checker Club* was probably not all that different from gaming groups today: people play their games with passion and meet others with similar interests. At the club, the players played fast and good, so everyone got great practice. My brother Roy spent many hours at the *Checker Club*, and he was a great checker player. Roy went to a lot of tournaments, and he became the state checker champion!

Back then there were three rows of parking on Central Avenue: one row of parking on each side pulling right up front of the business and one row right down the middle; this arrangement left just two narrow driving lanes, one going south, one going north. Jim Cleary (who at that time was 85 years old), told me about when the brick streets were laid around 1915. At that time, Jim was the Street Commissioner.

I remember the pride in his voice as he told of how this crew of black men came into town and laid those brick streets. He told of how precise they were in seeing that they had a perfect layer of sand to lie in, how they "eyeballed" the crest needed to be sure the water would drain into the gutters and not sit in puddles to soak in the lower sand and weaken it, that when everything was perfect, more sand was poured into the cracks between the bricks.

The bricks were made at the *Hawk Yard Brickyard*, located on Avenue A where the Kearney Catholic School is today. They had a big pit there where they dug in deep to mine the dense clay soil. Most the bricks around town were made locally with the good clay soil found here.

Richard "Dick" Dyer, lawyer and philosopher. During these years after college, I came back into contact with my seventh grade geography teacher, Richard Dyer. During the Second World War, he went into the service and got a commission as an officer. After the war, he went back to college on the GI bill and became a lawyer. He opened a general practice office on the corner of Avenue D near downtown.

Richard was quite a philosopher. I could go in and sit down and talk with him about a legal proposition I needed to talk with him about, and we would get into a conversation and he would go on and on about the most interesting of topics. Richard had a remarkable view on just about any subject. However, his practice wasn't paying much of anything. Years later he told me there was a time when I'd have sold myself to anyone who wanted to pay me 400 dollars a month. Richard moved to Omaha and became a Federal Judge.

Airbase, chickens. It had been a couple years since taking the accounting class, yet I still couldn't find long-term employment of any value or real future. So I took a job vaccinating chickens. There were two guys who started raising chickens out at the airbase where there were all the old barrack buildings and such. And they had rented these buildings. One of the guys was Mark McAllister; he was a local veterinarian. And the other entrepreneur was Cecil Coates; I think he was from Hastings. Anyway, they had these thousands of chickens they would bring in as baby chicks. They warmed up the buildings with wood stoves until the chicks got bigger.

Mark hired me to vaccinate the chickens. I had a crew of three guys helping me, and we had a system for working fast and efficiently. We'd go into a building and use old screen doors as panels to herd all the chickens to one end of the building. Then we would set up a box in between the screen partitions. I'd have one guy on my left and one on my right. Then the other guy would be out in the area we had blocked off, and he would be catching chickens and putting them in the little basket in between us. Each one of the guys beside me would pick up a chicken out of the basket, hold a leg up, and I would shoot them with vaccine. We released the vaccinated chickens on the open side of the panels, and then they grabbed more out of the basket. We inoculated the chickens against New Castle disease.

I don't know how many thousands of chickens I vaccinated, but I always used to say that I've looked at more chicken's asses than anyone in the world. Everybody there made the same money of 35 cents an hour. This was adequate pay for me since I was still single, living at home, and didn't have any expenses to speak of. Some employees would make more than their wages by stealing chickens and taking them home to eat.

Part time jobs.. Around this time I joined the Eagles Club. Very seldom would I drink at the Eagles Club. I just had no desire to drink. Instead I'd go down there and we'd play poker. These were limit games of ten and 25-cent limits, but many times I could win 35 dollars a week.

At one point, the secretary of the Eagles Club got in some kind of trouble over his bookkeeping, and they fired him. So the trustees hired me as a temporary secretary. That paid me 15 cents a member a month.

In the meantime, I got connected with an insurance company in Lincoln called Union Insurance. My district manager was a fellow by the name of Rowe. I sold mainly automobile and liability insurance for them since that's about all the insurance people bought in those days. They set me up and I would write business and house fire insurance and car and liability insurance for Union Insurance. I also wrote for Grain Dealers Mutual. So I started this little insurance business that never did make me much money.

Acting as a notary public is yet another part-time job I had at this time. A geologist from Kansas by the name of Armstrong hired me as his personal notary public.   I carried along my notary public seal, and he paid me a dollar an hour to ride along with him out in the country. Armstrong was a bit of an entrepreneur in that he went around to the country farms and homesteads and tried to get people to lease their ground oil rights. Armstrong would get a whole block of people to lease, and then he'd turn around and sell the group to a big oil company. I don't think those companies drilled on any of those leases.

George Sobotka, bookkeeping, 1949. One day I got a call from George Sobotka, asking me to come and work for him as a bookkeeper. Our families had been friends for years, so George thought of me when he needed to hire someone part-time to help with the bookkeeping at his business. George and Maxine Sobotka had a little filling station and garage they called George's Super Service. It sat near Central Avenue facing north onto Lincoln Highway. The parking lot for the Museum of Nebraska Art (MONA) is there now. The station had two gasoline pumps out front and three or four main mechanics in the back who worked on cars; George also sold GMC pickups.

Maxine showed me how to keep the books. There wasn't any accounting to it; it was just bookkeeping. I found out later that Maxine was pregnant with their second child, and they wanted someone else to do the bookwork while she was raising the two kids, Joe and Anna.

I started out working for him afternoons, and the pay was 75 cents an hour. I was selling insurance at the time, but I wasn't very good at it and being in my early twenties, living at home, I found it harder and harder to make myself get up in the mornings. So I asked George if I could work in the mornings so I'd have to get up. He agreed.

Every month had to balance out, and George wanted to know how much he made that month. This one month I had all the figures down and I showed him the end of the month.

He looked at the totals thoughtfully and finally he said, "Bubby that ain't right. There's something wrong here."

So I went back to the books, and I wondered how could he know that by just looking at the bottom line? I went back and redid everything and sure enough, George was right. I had made a mistake in my figures.

George was one of the smartest businessmen I ever met. He only had an eighth grade education, but that didn't keep him from being a hell of a businessman. I learned a lot from George.

Me with my Bothers, Roy & Art

Me Feeding Pigeons

25th & Central 1963

George had a clear-cut way of keeping books—just a simple single line of accounting to keep track of all the expenses and income and at the bottom of the page was your profit. George always paid for everything up front, so that added to the simplicity of it all. If the mechanics were working on a car and needed a carburetor or switch or something, they'd check out money from the cash register drawer. Usually they'd go across the street to Bearman Auto Electric and pay for a part, bring it back, and attach the receipt to the back of the work order for that particular job. George would mark it up a bit, and then tack on the labor charges. But on the back he always knew exactly what his costs were.

We always checked the cash every night and one night it was 20 dollars short.

I always remember him saying to me, "Bubby, I know that money didn't just fly out of there."

We looked all over trying to figure out where those 20 dollars went.

The next day when I came in, George said, "You know Bubby, I figured out where those 20 dollars went. I bought an engine from Leonard McKean and I forgot to get a receipt for it."

So that was our joke we always had with George. We might tease him and say, "Hey George, the till is 20 short. Did you buy another engine from McKeans?"

He'd grin at our teasing, and we'd all laugh in fun, all the while knowing George was one of the most intelligent businessmen you could ever meet.

Notice the Super Service Station in the upper right.

Being located right on the Lincoln Highway and downtown, the Super Service stayed a busy place and employed several others besides myself. Laurence Geiger ran the front desk and the filling station; most people called him Larry.   The station had three main mechanics at the time I was working there: Vern Capps, Bill Lemke, and Bob Lynch.   Bob came to work there after I started working there. George needed another mechanic, and I knew Bob was having some trouble making any money running the Sinclair station out on west Highway 30.

Bob and I were friends, so I asked, "Why don't you come in and talk to George about working at the station." Bob talked to George, and he hired Bob right away.

I always remember Bob smoked cigarettes. Of course his hands were oily and wet from working on parts, and that cigarette would get greasy and damp. Pretty soon that cigarette attached to his bottom lip and stuck there. Then the cigarette burned down to nothing and just the paper hung there. And Bob would talk, and there'd be that flat, brown paper cigarette butt stuck to his lip, riding up and down, as though it was supposed to be there. That was Bob. Bob's son, Dan Lynch, is now the Kearney Chief of Police.

Busy Times. So I'm working at George's filling station keeping books in the mornings, riding along with Mr. Armstrong notarizing oil leases in the afternoons, secretary of Eagles Club, selling insurance, and keeping books for Daryl Skyles Plumbing and Roeder Bros. Construction in my spare time (they didn't take much time since they were just starting in business) . Then several nights a week I played poker. I kept track for a while, and I was making over 35 dollars a week playing poker—making more money than I made with pay for all three bookkeeping jobs.

But gradually I got out of playing poker much, sold off my insurance agency, and they didn't re-elect me as secretary of the Eagles Club.

Beverly Jean Nelson. I met Beverly at the Eagle's Club. Her parents used to bring her with them on Saturday night. We met and fell in love right away. And on New Year's Eve we planned a June wedding. Beverly also had a handicap; she was very hard of hearing. When she didn't have her hearing aids on, she was almost deaf. But she didn't let that stop her from enjoying and participating in life to the fullest. She really enjoyed music, as she felt very deeply the vibrations of each note, each instrument. For high school, she attended the school for the deaf in Omaha.

So we were a good match for several reasons. For one, Beverly understood the challenges of having to find a way to do things in life that others might do without a second thought. Secondly, Beverly understood scarcity. I came from a poor family, but Beverly came from a family even more poor than my own!

And she accepted a life with me that was anything but rewarding. Few women would have put up with me while I was busy building the business. She was raised having nothing, and this gave her the ability to do without any luxuries. She did her thing trying to raise the four kids the best she could; it was tough on her and the kids those first ten years. I would be amiss if I didn't give Beverly some recognition as to any success I might achieve.

Birthday Suit. On one of my birthdays, Beverly bought me a suit at Hirshfield's Clothing downtown. She said that if I didn't like it, I could exchange it for something else. I already had a brown suit, so I took it back and picked out some other clothes. Then some months later I was looking in the closet, and there was that new brown suit! Immediately I knew that I'd taken back my old brown suit, which was covered in plastic from the drycleaners, to the store. I took the new brown suit back and asked Mr. Hirshfield why he didn't call me.

He smiled and said, "I knew you'd figure it out."

When my daughter Lynda was born, I played poker and won enough to pay the 50-dollar hospital bill. I used to laugh and tease Lynda, telling everyone: "I won Lynda in a poker game."

Beverly and me with our first two kids, Lynda and Mike.

Whitney Sand & Gravel full time. Then along after I'd worked for George a couple years, Carl Whitney offered me a full time job with him and Whitney Sand & Gravel. I ran the office at the sand pit and kept books for 60 dollars a week. This position actually involved keeping up several different books for the various business enterprises.   First there was work with a personal account for Carl Whitney and an individual account for Wert Whitney. Then there was Whitney Sand and Gravel, which was a partnership between Bill Whitney, Carl Whitney and Vern Broadfoot. Then there was Carl Whitney, the contractor. Carl had contracting jobs away from Kearney about any place he could find a job. Then there was the company of Whitney and Richter. Carl had an employee named Ernie Richter, and he took Ernie in as his partner in land leveling and moving equipment; they used Carl's big heavy-duty lowboy to move equipment.

I worked there for two or three years. I learned a lot about business in those years. Carl's dad Wert Whitney sat in the office off in one quarter. Wert owned the land used by Whitney Sand & Gravel. We became friends, and he would tell me stories and memories. He told me that he used to sit on the raft and pump sand and gravel, and he'd dream of having a steak house on the sand pit. Later on he moved a building from the airbase and turned it into a steak house. They called it Grandpa's Steak House.

Part 2: The life & growth of a company and a man

ACE IRRIGATION

1957 meeting Ace Irrigation. One day I picked up some stamps in the Post Office, and Ace Gallup was in there. Some years earlier I met Ace at an auction, and then occasionally I would see him around town. Ace struck up a conversation with me and wanted to know what I was doing. I told him that I was working for Whitneys as a bookkeeper.

At one point he mentioned that he was looking for a bookkeeper for his company, Ace Irrigation. Finally he jumped in and asked, "Well, how'd you like to come to work for me?"

I smiled. "I kind of enjoy where I'm working now."

"What are you making there?"

"I'm making 60 dollars a week."

Ace looked at me with determined steel gray eyes and smiled. "I'll pay you 100 dollars a week to come to work for me keeping the books."

My heart raced, and I thought to myself, "Wow, that's five grand a year!" That's a lot of money. So I went to work for Ace, doing books for him. That was 1957, and we had a pretty good year.

He hired me to keep books, but it wasn't very long and I was selling pipe and equipment to farmers. So I wasn't only keeping books, but also I was salesman too. I really didn't know too much about what I was doing, but I could sell.

The original Ace Irrigation building sat on the corner of Avenue Q and Highway 30.

I remember this one time when I'd sold this pretty good-sized order to this farmer, and Ace looked at the ticket, and obviously impressed, he asked, "Did you make that sale?"

"Yea, Ace I did."

"Well," he said, "We must be selling stuff too cheap. We better raise the price."

But we didn't really raise the prices; they stayed the same. I continued to sell. And I continued to learn about the business.

Asa Gallup. Asa Gallup, nicknamed "Ace," grew up around Exeter, Nebraska. Then he moved to Shelton, then Gibbon and finally the Kearney area. Early in his work career, Ace had a corn sheller, and he shelled corn for farmers. He told me that he shelled corn all day, and then he'd work half the night fixing the machine up so he could shell corn the next day. In those days they picked the corn on the ear, and then they stored it until the corn sheller came in and shelled the corn off the cob. He did that for many years.

Then he came to Kearney and bought a little piece of ground there on East 25th Street. The building sat on the corner of Avenue Q and Highway 30. During WWII he started selling cultivators and the like—not tractors or anything like that, but implements. They called it G-I Implement. Government Issue registered it as General Implement Company. They had all kinds of attachments for tractors to use for farming. Sometime after the war, he had a sale and just sold out everything and retired. But Ace kept the property on Highway 30.

Ace Irrigation opens. In 1952 Ace became restless and decided to start an irrigation company. He named it Ace Irrigation. He bought aluminum pipe from the west coast and sold it for irrigation pipe. At this time these were hand move pipe sprinkler lines. And in those days it was mostly extruded aluminum pipe, not pipe made on a tube mill as we make today. He would buy a railroad boxcar load of mostly three, four, five and six inch pipe. And he would buy couplers and ends for them. Later on he made his own couplers and ends.

I worked for Ace through 1957, and then in 1958 it rained and it rained and it rained. There was just no business. At that time Ace had two gals working for him in the office, Rose Bishop and Marie Coral. With Ace and me, that made four of us in the office and no business. I could see the handwriting on the wall.

One day I went to Ace and said, "You know Ace, this is kind of ridiculous. You've got all these people in the office and there just isn't any business. Whitneys have asked me to come back and pay me the same amount of money you're paying me. And so why don't I go back to work for Whitneys? I could still do books for you in the evening if you want me to."

Ace agreed that's the thing to do. So I went back to work for Whitneys. That was in 1958.

Ace Irrigation with company stock. Then about a year later, Ace came to talk with me.   He'd lost both gals in the office. Marie Coral moved away, and Rose didn't really know that much about bookkeeping in the first place.   So he approached me about coming back to do bookkeeping for him.

"I'll give you 100 dollars a week," He said.   "We'll incorporate and I'll sell you stock in the company. You pay me 40 dollars a month out of your wages, and then you'll get 20 percent of the profits we make."

His proposal looked like something with some future in it, so I quit Whitneys and went back to work for Ace Irrigation.

Commercials. As part of an advertising campaign for business, Ace staged TV commercials during the evening news on Channel 13. Usually he had two commercials, each lasting a minute. In one commercial, Ace banged on an aluminum coupler to get your attention and to show the strength of aluminum.

"We should cut the hammer in half," I suggested, "and then when you hit the aluminum coupler the hammer would break."

We tried it. But when Ace started banging on the coupler, the hammer blew into two pieces and almost hit a 400,000-dollar camera! We didn't do that again.

In another commercial, Ace and his salesman, Emmett Crawford, had a 50-gallon barrel filled with corn. At the bottom they had a suction fan hooked to a gas engine. They cut up some crepe paper and put it in the top of the barrel to move around to show the air moving through the barrel. But they spent the whole minute segment, trying to get the motor started. They just kept pulling the cord over and over for what turned into a very long minute. After the commercial was over, they realized they forgot to turn the petcock valve open to let the gas in to start the engine.

As time went on, I took over doing the commercials for the business. We had a dealer in Goodland, Kansas, Dean Topliff, and we did some commercials on their little TV station down there. We set up that dealership in a filling station, and our commercials advertised the office there. Dean was a good dealer and sold a lot of pipe down there out of that filling station office.

Ace Gallup and me.

Ace had a very inventive mind, and he was always trying to think of something to make a dollar.

74

Channel 13. Down at the Channel 13 station, there was quite a fun group working together. The cameraman was Dick Larson—who later became the Chief Deputy Sheriff. One of the newscasters was Mo Milligan, and the sportscaster was Jerry Granger. They were always messing around, pulling jokes of some kind. One evening when I was there, Mo pulled one on Jerry. Jerry was reading his sports notes live, and Mo stuck a bulletin in Jerry's notes saying:

NEWS FLASH BULLETIN: Everyone rush to the Holdrege Airport!

There's a seaplane that needs to land down there.

Everyone bring a bucket of water—quick!

Jerry didn't fall for it, but everyone got a good laugh.

Ace business 59, 60, 61. Unfortunately, the irrigation business wasn't very good during the years '59, '60 and '61. But Ace had a very inventive mind, and he was always trying to think of something to make a dollar.

We were already selling perforated aluminum pipe to farmers to put in their grain bin to keep air moving through the grain to preserve it. So we started making suction fans to suck air through the grain—known as aeration. The farmer lays perforated pipe in the bottom of the grain bin and hooks the suction fan to it. When he turns on the fan, the fan pulls air through the grain, sucks it into the perforated pipe, and releases the hot air out into the environment. Some of our fans ran on gasoline and some ran on electricity.

Then we started making little three foot long rotary grain cleaners. We welded 20-inch tire rims together, put a screen inside, and set them at an angle. Then we attached a small electric motor. The farmer set it on top of a grain bin, and the screen turned, throwing the chaff and impurities off into the air, while letting the clean grain fall into the bin. And it did a good job for the farmer.

ACE IRRIGATION EQUIPMENT CO.,
KEARNEY, NEBR.
FEBR. 28, 1959

	4,218.92	4,545.89
Cash on Hand		
Cash in Bank	15,476.34	
Accounts Receivable	1,661.64	
Notes Receivable	41,741.75	5,440.78
Inventory	12,309.49	
Equipment--Shop & Misc		3,669.20
Reserve for Deprec Shop & Misc	6,265.00	
Equipment--Trucks		1,130.57
Reserve for Deprec Truck	2,581.45	
Equipment--Office		185.39
Reserve for Deprec Office	223.22	
Prepaid Insuracne		8,825.55
Accounts Payable	5,000.00	54.70
Notes Payable		69.66
Customer Deposits		81,980.12
Social Security Tax Payable		
Withholding Tax Payable		19,988.01
Capital Investement	20,535.50	7,288.26
Asa Gallup Personal Draw		755.01
Irrigation Sales		
Dryer & Grain Storage		
Miscellaneous Sales	656.51	
Office Labor	1,644.34	
Shop Labor	18,718.06	
Materials & Supplies	198.00	
T V. Advertising	20.69	
Newspaper Advertising	27.48	
Miscellaneous Advertising	22.77	
Dealer & Customer Entertainment	33.14	
Freight	286.95	
Taxes & License	78.63	
Gas & Oil	60.00	
Truck Rental	42.30	
Salesman Taveling Expenses	45.83	
Office Supplies & Expense	13.50	
Stamps & Postage	42.20	
Lights	26.48	
Heat	42.63	
Telpehone & Telegraph	561.94	
Insurance	164.35	
Travel Expense by owner	68.00	
Dues & Subscriptions	3.90	
Outside Labor	57.50	
Lot Rental	724.65	
Refunds & Merchandise Returned	57.52	
Social Security Tax Co. Share	225.71	
Real Estate Tax	93.30	
Bad Debts	1.45	
Miscellaneous Expense	133,933.14	133,933.14

Balance Sheet

"Ace Irrigation Equipment Co.

Kearney, Nebr.

Febr. 28, 1959"

Ace got the idea that if this was good for the farmer, then we should make a big one for the elevators. Emmett Crawford was working for him by that time as a salesman, and Ace and Emmett thought these grain cleaners were going to be great for the grain dealer.

I was of the opinion that the elevators don't want to spend a bunch of time and expense cleaning the grain. The grain dealers could actually make more money by not cleaning the grain. When the grain dealer bought the farmer's grain, they would not pay premium price for premium grain, but they'd pay a discounted price for dirty or low quality grain. Then they'd mix the good grain and the bad grain together and sell it all at the higher premium price.

Ace stubbornly disagreed with me, and they built two of these great big monstrous, rolling grain cleaners. And they never did sell a one.

Sell back stock. We got into a real disagreement about those huge fans. And it got to the point when we were just not getting along at all about a lot of things.

I went to Ace and said, "Look this is not working. Why don't I just sell back my company stock, and then you guys can just go ahead and do whatever you want and we won't have this big conflict all the time. I'll go on keeping books for you as long as you want me to, but we're in such a disagreement that I don't think it'll work for us to be partners."

By this time I'd accumulated a good amount of worth in the company, counting the 40 dollars a month, adding the 20 percent profit of the other years--which didn't amount to much, anyway, and the total came to around five grand. So Ace agreed, and he paid me off for my share of the business.

This was 1961. I still continued to work there even though Ace and I were not really on the best of speaking terms.

On the home front. I took that 5000 dollars and bought a different house for my growing family.

Until this time we lived in a little house on East 26th Street that was once a chicken coop. I bought the chicken coop house from Art and Max Liesienger on a farm south of Gibbon. They'd done some work on it converting it from chicken coup to house. I paid 300 dollars for it, and 300 dollars for the lot in Kearney. I had Bill Gant pour the floor and lay the block for the basement.

To say there wasn't much room is an understatement. The chicken coop house had an open area in the middle and front for the kitchen and living room. I added a room-like porch on the back that served as the only bedroom for all of us. And there were six of us by this time, with me and my wife Beverly, along with our four kids, Lynda, Mike, LeAnn, and Dick, ages eight, five, four, and one respectively. In our bedroom was one double bed, a set of bunk beds and a crib. Always the budding entrepreneur, Bev and I raised tropical fish in old glass battery jars in the little basement.

There was an auction house just a couple doors down from the chicken coop house. My folks, now Grandpa and Grandma Thomas would go to that auction. Grandma looked for salt and pepper shakers to add to her collection. And Grandpa loved to visit with others at the auction. Grandma wrote her shopping lists on a rainbow tablet, and many times they'd both go home for a lunch of bread and gravy.

Accident on the road. A serious accident occurred while we lived at the chicken coop house. The summer day arrived, the same as countless other sunny summer days for the kids. On this day a bunch of the neighborhood kids gathered at the giant slide over on Avenue N. The slide was quite tall and had a number of lanes. Sometimes, the man who owned it let the neighborhood kids ride for free if they'd wax it for him. He'd give them big sheets of wax paper to ride down the slide, while the paying customers rode down on burlap sacks.

Lynda, Mike and sometimes LeAnn would go to the slide together with neighborhood friends. As they walked home that day, Mike crossed the street to look for bugs in a vacant field. Before he could make it across the street, though, a car sped around the corner and hit Mike. Making matters worse, the driver slammed on the brakes at just the wrong moment, and Mike's left leg caught underneath the tire, grinding the leg into the gravel. He was significantly injured and taken to the hospital. The doctors just barely managed to save Mike's leg.

While Mike was still in a cast we moved to our home at 1902 Avenue D. This sturdy old house constructed of heavy blocks had three bedrooms upstairs for the kids, and a playroom and bedroom on the main floor. It seemed like a castle! But for the first few weeks at the new house, Mike lay in a hospital bed in front of the dining room bay window.

Sugar cubes with a purpose. Around this time, the fight against polio improved with the development of vaccines. The first vaccine available was Dr. Jonas Salk's dead-virus vaccine. This vaccine required an injection. To finally have something for this battle was great news! The 1950's were particularly bad, with 1952 a standout year with around 60,000 cases of polio and about 3,000 deaths in the US alone. Dr. Albert Sabin developed a live-virus oral vaccine. Sabin's oral vaccine became the most widely used of the two vaccines, due partly to the ease of use. Salk's vaccine needed an injection while Sabin's oral vaccine was dropped on a sugar cube for easy and tasty ingestion.

There were mass inoculations across the US. Many times they gave the doses at whatever place could hold a line of people. Around Kearney they gave the vaccine at various locations including the schools, and I believe they gave doses out at the County Extension Office.

As a family, we went to Bryant School in south Kearney where we lined up to get the little sugar cube that carried a big message for the polio virus. The whole country breathed a collective sigh of relief to have some hope against this virus that ravaged uncontrolled for decades. For me, this sigh of relief hit me personally as I looked at my innocent children, now the ages I was when struck with the paralysis brought on by polio.

 "This medicine will help you so you don't get polio," I said to my young kids. "And then you won't get sick and have to wear crutches like me."

Even though I already had polio, I could contract a different type of the virus. So I took an oral dose in a sugar cube as well, since the vaccine offered protection from all three types of polio. A number of people fell victim to polio—twice. They would get one type and then get another type.

"Let Ace make your pipe dreams come true"

Tucson. At one point, Ace and his wife Billie went down to Tucson, Arizona to visit their son Alan. Alan had set up a dental practice down there. They stayed there for a few weeks. Billie had respiratory problems, and they soon realized that she could breathe much better down there than she could here—and they found out they loved Arizona. So when Ace came back he announced that he was going to sell the company, retire, and move to Arizona.

For sale. Ace searched and searched and tried everybody he could think possible to take the business over, but he just couldn't find anyone that wanted to buy this business.   It didn't amount to much at the time. For instance in 1958 total gross sales totaled only 87,000 dollars. Once we paid out the expenses, the company didn't have any money left. And business was the same for '60 and '61. Ace thought the irrigation business was over.

Towards the end of 1961, Sam Porter, a mutual friend of both Ace and me, suggested that Ace sell it to me on contract.

"Sell it to Lynn," Sam told Ace, "and then you can retire and move down there. And if it doesn't work out, you can always come back and take it over again."

So they came to me, and Ace said that he'd like to sell the business to me.

Ace wanted 150,000 dollars for the business and that would include the land and the building. I said that I couldn't go to that extent. And besides, there wasn't any inventory to speak of.   The building was nothing but an old filling station covered in aluminum siding. The whole place was about ready to fall to pieces and full of termites. Finally they came to a value of 75,000 dollars for the kit and caboodle.   So that was the contract, and I was supposed to pay him 40 dollars a month for ten years.

The new owner. I took over ownership of Ace Irrigation on the first day of January in 1962. I had no money, no real assets, and I had the responsibility of a wife and four kids.

Well as soon as I took over the company, my first thought was how to manage the money part. Plain and simple: I needed more funds for operating.

Harold Oldfather. So I went to First National Bank and paid a visit to my banker, Harold Oldfather.

I said, "Harold, I only have a 50,000 dollar line of credit, and I need an additional 25,000 dollar line of credit. I just can't operate on only the 50,000 dollar line in credit."

"No," Harold said, "I just can't go that high for you, Lynn. You just don't have enough equity."

"Would you mind if I shop around and see if I can find a bank that'll back me?"

"No, that'll be fine," Harold said, and we shook hands.

Years later I got a phone call out of the blue from Harold. He took me out to lunch. As we talked about old times, Harold told me that one of the greatest regrets of his life is not backing me on that loan when I needed him. His words touched me deeply, and it was one of the greatest compliments I could remember receiving.

Bob Rapp. After talking with Harold, I went home and slept on it. I find that if I sleep on it, my subconscious mind works on the problem. The next morning I woke up, and I thought about Bob Rapp, a customer in Norcatur, Kansas. Bob managed a grain company, and he bought a lot of perforated aluminum pipe for aeration. And I had become good friends with Bob, selling to him over the years I worked for Ace.

So I went down to Norcatur and met with Bob. "You know here's the story," I said. "I bought this business, and I need more operating capital. Is there any possibility that we could work out a deal, and you could advance me 15,000 dollars on future purchases?"

Bob agreed to do just that! In fact he did that for four years straight. Every January I'd go down there and pick up a check for fifteen grand. That help was the beginning of good things to come. So I owe a debt of gratitude for that.

That money from Bob helped tide me over until I found a bank that could back me for more than 50,000 dollars.

Ron. Well, I looked around for a while and finally found a young banker by name of Ron Bycroft at the Gibbon Exchange Bank. He was a real go-getter of a banker. And he was looking for accounts he could work with. Ron gave me the credit line I needed, and his faith in me became instrumental in helping the business grow.

Gated Irrigation pipe. Right after I bought the business, gated irrigation pipe became very popular. Ace thought the irrigation business was gone and wouldn't come back. But these farmers came out of the walls clamoring to buy gated pipe, and all of a sudden there was all this business—it seemed everyone wanted to go into gated pipe!

Historically, it was time for a change in irrigation. In the 1930's farmers started using lathe boxes to irrigate. The boxes were made from used lathe boards, nailed together to form a box about two inches in diameter. The farmer would stick the box in the side of the irrigation ditch, run water down the ditch, and water would run through the box and into the crop row.

Around 1945 farmers saw plastic siphon tubes introduced for a lighter, more efficient way of getting water out of the ditch and down the crop row. The farmer placed this uniquely shaped tube in the ditch water, and it curved over the ditch edge. Water siphoned through the tube, over the edge and into the row. This simple but effective system continued in use by some for decades. However, with ditch irrigation there is a lot of wasted water through evaporation and seepage into the ground along the way. Ditches could break causing more water loss and more labor for repairs. On top of that was the backbreaking, endless labor all day, all summer. These obstacles called for something better.

In the fifties a few farmers started using gated pipe for irrigation, but then about the time I bought the business, gated pipe really took off in popularity.

As a metal, aluminum offered the right combination of being lightweight but sturdy. Generally, each length of pipe was 30 foot long with couplers on the end to attach each length together. I made a connection with Kroy Metal in York and Midwest Irrigation in Henderson, buying pipe from them.

First Employees. When I bought the company, I had hardly any help. There was me, one full time employee in the shop, one part-time in the office and one part-time in the shop—quite a skeleton crew.

Out in the shop area Willsey Krutz, a machinist, worked full time on anything and everything needed.

In the 1950s Ace had developed an 8" female coupler. He also had a mold made to make the couplers.

Chuck. Chuck Wood worked in the summer welding couplers on pipe. In the early years he had a drinking problem, and sometimes he parked on the east side of the building and slept it off. I would wake him up when it was time to go to work. But Chuck was one very bright person. If I wanted something made, I would tell Chuck, and the next day it would be there for me. Chuck was the one person I could always count on. In honor of this great man, we have a concrete drive circling out and around north of our present buildings that we named Chuck Wood drive. Of all the people who worked for me, Chuck had a great deal to do with the beginning of Ace Irrigation. Chuck had a brilliant mind, and he was self-educated. He knew such things as trigonometry. I could ask him to build anything, to do anything, and he built it. Despite his weakness for alcohol, he did stop drinking and became the right hand man in the manufacturing side of the business.

Vi. Our truck driver was Vi Aborgast, a burly, robust woman with copper red hair and a bold yet sweet nature. She stood about six feet tall with heavy bones to match. Physically she could match most men out there. In the beginning, she mostly delivered out to the farms in the Kearney area. As we expanded, she delivered out into Kansas, Wyoming, and Colorado to farms and some dealerships. On a trip to Wyoming the State Patrol pulled her over. The patrolman explained that he'd never seen a woman truck driver, so he had to pull her over and see for himself close up.

Once Vi hauled some pipe to a farm owned by two bachelors.

After unloading the pipe, one farmer asked, "Are you married?"

Vi laughed and said, "yes."

"That's too bad," said the farmer. "We could sure use a woman like you here on the farm."

Ed Louis, a Sergeant with the Kearney Police Department, also hauled pipe for us on his days off.

At that time I bought plain pipe. Then I'd hire four or five high school teenagers in the summer to run the jig out in the shop, cutting gate holes. A few of these teens include, Scott Morris, Ron Larson, Joe Sobotka, and Kenny Eichenburg. These were some I remember, but there were many, many others. Scott owns Morris Press, an innovative press and publishing company located just over a stone's throw down the highway from Ace Irrigation. And Ron and Joe certainly put their marks in Kearney as well.

Kenny became a state patrolman. One summer after working for me for four years, Kenny came into the office, smiling sheepishly. "I lied to you when I came to work for you," he said. "I was actually only 13 years old—and not 16 years old as I put on my application!"

In those days you could legally run a router and be 16 years old. Today you must be 18 years old to handle any kind of equipment. And Kenny was only 13 years old!

Mac. Nineteen sixty-two was a great year. I made some money that year! So I just had to have more help. I looked around and I remembered a guy by the name of Mac McClemens. Al Ingram had a great business at Kearney Foundry, and Mac used to work there. But he quit them. Mac bought an old sawmill out in the country near what is now the Minden Interchange on I-80. He spent his days sawing lumber. He was selling some and building a house with that lumber.

I got to wondering if Mac would be interested in working for me. I went out to his place, and he was very excited about coming to work for me. So Mac came to work for me, and he was a hell of a salesman. He liked to work all night. But then when he got up in the morning, he could look and act cranky as mad bull. But boy he could burn the midnight oil with the best of them and get a lot done. You just didn't want to be a bucket around Mac in the mornings because he'd kick you across the field if you were in his way.

License plates. I had a couple tricks to help me in the office. One trick helped me with knowing customer names. I wanted to be friendly and knowledgeable to my customers. So I wanted to greet them by name when they walked in. But I couldn't remember every customer's name. I might've only see them once before. My desk was by the front window so I could see them pull up—and I could see their license plate. So I started writing down license plate numbers and putting that number on a card. Then when they pulled up the next time, I'd quickly look in my card box and see who they were. When they stepped in, I'd be ready with a friendly, "Well, hi John, how are you doing?"

Telephone Switch. Another trick that helped me occurred with the phone. I talked to General Telephone and arranged to have the company phone ring at my house whenever I left the office for home.

General Telephone had a big switchboard downtown, and they installed a switch on my telephone line at the office. Then in the evening when I left the office, I just flipped that switch.   Then the business phone would ring at my home phone, and I wouldn't miss any business calls. Most people will chuckle when they hear about this "great and wonderful invention" from the phone company. Today call forwarding seems natural and almost insignificant given the unlimited features on a smart phone. But back then, my little switch was quite on the cutting edge.

Mike, Dick, Lynda, LeAnn

Dangerous drives. Sometimes necessity called for me to drive under dangerous conditions.

One weekend I loaded up the family, and we drove over to Spitz Foundry in Hastings. I bought an old welder truck for 800 dollars. I needed that truck out in the field when we wanted to weld steel pipe together for underground projects. For the ride back to Kearney, my son Mike rode with me in the truck and Bev drove the station wagon with the other kids.

That truck being a stick shift and all the joints a little too loose from age, it could be a slippery drive for about anyone, but it was downright dangerous for me. I had severely limited strength in my left leg and foot with virtually no push power at all. My right leg and foot were weak as well, and a thick, clunky built up shoe on my right foot further hampered my driving. So everything I did was like running my legs on manual power.

 Just like driving a stick shift back in my college days, I ran through the multi-step motions of simply putting on the brakes:

   1) with my left hand, lift my left leg up and put it on the clutch
   2) push my left leg down on the clutch
   3) kick it out of gear with my right hand (gear shift is on the floor)
   4) grab the emergency brake and pull it back and lock it
   5) reach down and pick up my right leg and put it on the brake
   6) with my right hand push my right leg down on the brake
   7) all the while, my hands are switching back and forth off and on the steering wheel.

Changing gears was just about as complicated with lots of picking up and putting down in a short period of time. So needless to say, driving the welding truck pushed the whole procedure to my limits. Certainly, no fast stops could be expected. So with a hope and a prayer we made it home—only to repeat the circumstances a couple months later, a little bit louder and a little bit worse.

Fourth of July 1963. I got an order for a trailer load of aeration pipe for Norcatur, Kansas. And I couldn't find anyone to drive the truck down there. Mike climbed up in the truck with me, and we headed for Kansas. The truck was a Chevy dooly stick shift, which was sort of okay for me to drive. But add a heavy load of pipe behind it, along with my physical challenges, and quick braking becomes something close to impossible. But away we went. I did drive with extreme caution, but I shutter when I look back at how dangerous that was, especially on a holiday.

We made it safely to Kansas and delivered our load. On the way home, we stopped on the Kansas line and bought fireworks.

Mike remembers, "I was so excited we were going to Kansas! It was every young kid's dream to get to go to Kansas and buy real firecrackers like Black Cats. We also got some high-powered bottle rockets and Roman candles. In Nebraska we could only buy little bitty firecrackers like Ladyfingers."

Lynda, LeAnn and Dick also enjoyed the Kansas fireworks, which were most likely illegal in Nebraska.

I was a dreamer. I guess I picked that up from Ace Gallup. My mind was always alert. And most evenings I came home from a hectic day and I was thinking so much that I couldn't get to sleep. So I manufactured a way to get some sleep: I imagined building a house. I poured the concrete, laid the blocks, and visualized what the house would be like. In the process of doing this, I relaxed, and bang, I'd be asleep. It got so once I started pouring the concrete, I'd go straight to sleep. I did build that house in 1967.

About the only family time was going for a drive on Sundays. We'd drive around in a big old station wagon, and I'd sing old songs like *Old Shep*. Sometimes we went to the A&W drive-in on east Hwy 30. We let the kids pick to have either a frosty mug of root beer or a soft serve ice cream cone. A&W chilled thick, heavy glass mugs, so your mug of root beer arrived cold and frosty. Occasionally on a summer evening, we'd have a big night and head out for a movie at the Kearney Drive-In on Avenue N. We popped popcorn, making enough to half fill a brown paper grocery sack. Then we picked up a gallon of A&W root beer in a glass jug, and off we went for a movie at the Drive-In.

During those times, we always said my daughter Lynda was my legs and her mom's ears. Since Bev couldn't hear well, and I couldn't always jump up quickly when needed, Lynda was the stand in at times. It was especially hard for Bev to hear on the phone, so young Lynda talked to the person on the phone and relayed the message to Bev. Lynda ran into the store for milk or bread and helped run after her younger siblings.

Dick was born mechanical and needing to tear things apart. Give Dick a screwdriver and a phone, and he'd be busy for hours tearing it apart. He once took out all the screws from the kitchen chairs. When we sat down for supper, all the chairs fell apart.

Mike clowned around and could always get LeAnn to laughing uncontrollably—many times at the wrong time and getting them both in trouble for being "wise guys". LeAnn liked reading, art and cooking. She used her Easy Bake oven to make me soft homemade pretzels.

There wasn't a lot of family time, but in the winter we'd play chess. While they were young, I taught all the kids to play chess. And during their grade school years, we'd have family chess tournaments on long winter weekends.

When we started making a little money, occasionally, we'd splurge and have dinner out at the Plain View Café on east Highway 30.

The kids remember, "You could always tell if Dad was really upset. He'd blow up and get to carrying on, and then he'd swing out his wooden crutch and then—whack! He'd slam the crutch on the side of his built up shoe, with a hollow wood-on-wood sound that scared the crap out of you."

And there were many memories of being out at Ace Irrigation as youngsters. They can all remember that first time they were told, "Don't look at the welder; it'll hurt your eyes."

Every couple of years after the hectic irrigation season, I'd give myself a little time off and take the family on vacation. Nothing fancy. On the trip, we'd rent motel rooms with a kitchenette and cook our meals right there. On one trip we visited my brothers who lived in California and Oregon. The kids remember that trip partly because they bought jeans not widely available in Nebraska at the time—bellbottom jeans.

1964 Business. When I first took ownership of Ace Irrigation, my future success looked questionable. I had no real assets, limited credit, and the irrigation business was slow in the couple years prior to me taking over the business. But thanks to the good Lord and the wonderful farmers of our community, sales increased. The farmers showered me with their business! And I made enough in the first two years to pay off the 75,000-dollar note on the business. I'm sure Ace was surprised at the success but happy to have his money.

LIVELIHOOD OVER THE YEARS

ACTIVITY	INCOME	EMPLOYER
Vaccinate Chickens	35 cents per hour	Coats & McAllister
Secretary in Real Estate Office	$15 per week	Jim Cleary, Ed Neustrom
Bookkeeping	75 cents per hour	George Sobotka
Eagles Club Secretary	15 cents per member per month	
Sell Insurance	Commission	
Play Poker at Night	25-cent limit	
Bookkeeping	$60 per week	Whitney Sand & Gravel
Bookkeeping & Sales	$100 per week	Ace Irrigation
Bookkeeping	$100 per week	Whitney Sand & Gravel
Bookkeeping, Sales, Part Owner	$100 per week	Ace Irrigation
	Plus 20 percent share of profits	
Owner Ace Irrigation	1962 Purchase Ace Irrigation for $75,000	
Owner Ace Irrigation	1964 Paid off note	

Idea for Tube mill. I got to thinking about having to buy all our pipe from other companies. So I thought, maybe I could buy a tube mill and make our own pipe!

I knew there was a machine shop down by Lincoln that made mills. And they gave me a quote for a mill that would make six to twelve inch diameter pipe. The shop, called Gordon & Morgan, was actually located in village of Havelock, which used to be near Lincoln. Today Havelock is gone, having long ago been absorbed into the city of Lincoln.

Then I went down to Gibbon and talked to my banker Ron Bycroft at the Exchange Bank.

"Ron, the real profit in this is the manufacture and selling of aluminum pipe," I said. "And there's a company in Lincoln that makes tube mills to make aluminum pipe. The mill I want would cost about 125,000 dollars. But I don't have that kind of credit line."

Ron, ever the optimist about me, said, "I can't loan it to you directly, but we'll find you the money."

Ron got to work on it, and he lined us up with talking to the bankers at Omaha National Bank. Omaha National was the big bank that was a corresponding bank to Ron's Gibbon Exchange Bank. We hoped they might back me on this big loan. Ron and I went down to Omaha a few times to talk with them. Finally, Ron talked them into backing me to buy the mill.

So we borrowed the money, and I ordered the mill. The mill I ordered would make 6, 8, 10, and 12-inch pipe. My nephew, Gordon Thomas worked for me, and I sent him down to Lincoln to be trained how to run it.

Ron had a little two-seater airplane, and he insisted on flying us to Omaha. So I tossed my crutches in the cockpit, and then I pulled myself across the wing and up into the plane. There is simply no way to climb or crawl very well with weak legs like mine. But most of the time when I met up with physical obstacles, like getting onto this plane, I'd manage to figure out some way to get past my limitations.

On the way to Omaha, Ron put the plane on autopilot, so the plane just quietly cruised along without any directions. We were sitting there visiting on the way, and then I realized Ron wasn't talking back. I glanced over and he wasn't moving.

My first panicked thought was "he's dead!" I nudged him a little, and he woke up with a surprised start. He'd dozed off while piloting the plane!

Still shaking, I yelled, "Don't you ever do that to me again!"

Lease buildings. I ordered the tube mill, but I had no place to put it. The little shop at my business location on east Highway 30 didn't have any room to speak of and certainly couldn't hold something as large and long as a tube mill.

So I looked around and found an empty building out at the airbase. This was a big old grey storage building left over from World War II when troops gathered here before shipping out. At one time, this one was used for corn storage. But it was empty now except for a bit of old corn in the corners. There were a number of such buildings out at the airport. The airport was on city property by this time, so I leased it from the city. And when the tube mill arrived, we moved it into that building.

What a great day when the tube mill was all assembled and ready to run. But honestly, we ran a lot of scrap aluminum when we first started. We had to get all the adjustments set just right or the aluminum would crinkle up as it went through the rollers. Fortunately, aluminum coil was only costing us 35 cents a pound, and we sold the scrap for 10 cents a pound. It was still a loss, but a manageable loss. Then once we got the mill tweaked and running reasonably well, we could really put out the pipe.

By that time, the next building to the east of that building became empty. So we leased that building too. And we built an office in the west end of that building. We moved the rest of the business from Highway 30 out to the airbase. We also put in a steel welding shop in the building with the tube mill. In the mean time a third building became empty, so we leased that building. Now we had three buildings all in a row. Each building was 50 foot wide by 200 feet long.

The aluminum pipe business was good. The farmers were making money and we were making the pipe. And I continued to pour profits back into the company.

We had a few dealers back then, and we've added many more over the years. The dealers mainly sold fittings, gates, gaskets and aluminum gated pipe. Ralph Kleveno is a dealer I had in Idalia, Colorado. He was a really good dealer, sold a lot of equipment. And of course there was Bob Rapp, General Manager of MGM Grain Company from Norcatur, Kansas. They sold aeration for us. Bob was generous enough to help us by prepaying for product in January each year. Then there was Bob Mapes from R.J. Mapes Manufacturing Company. He took over Air Master Aeration, manufacturing aeration fans. Bob made everything except the aeration tubing, so we'd sell him that. Then years later we sold him the equipment, so he could perforate the tubing in house.

Local lore. From the beginning we had wonderful customers who became great friends. I remember many, many customers and friends over the years. I hesitate to start naming them because there were so many of them, and I'd hate to miss one. There's just too many to try and write about them all, but they know who they are, and they know I appreciate them—everyone. They were all so good to me, and we sold them a lot of pipe.

I remember Kenny Denton, customer and friend. Kenny and Harold Oldfather were good friends. Kenny ran Harold's farms, and did a lot of business with us over the years. He was also a friend. Back then Kenny was also Superintendent of the Industrial School, now known as Youth Development Center or YDC. At one time people around here called it the "Boy's Training School." Whatever it's been called over the years, it has always been a place for boys in trouble.

In those days, the school had a little dairy and milked some cows. They also raised pigs and chickens and some beef. And every summer they had a huge garden in the area south of the school. The boys and young men at the school worked hard and also learned about agriculture. They not only raised food for the school, but they also raised food for all the local state institutions like the TB Hospital and Kearney State College.

Then sometime in the '60s, a superintendent came in and said we don't need to teach these kids to be farmers; they'll never be farmers. So he ended all the gardening and livestock. But what Kenny and others had known is that the farming was teaching the kids how to work, even if they never became farmers.

There used to be a filling station down the hill from the Industrial School gardens on Highway 30 that I believe was used for state cars and such.

Below: The original three buildings at the airport. The middle building has Ace Irrigation painted on the roof.

Right: Our first tube mill. My nephew, Gordon Thomas in the photo went to Lincoln to be trained in how to run it.

Lynn Thomas Is Named State Small Businessman of Year

Lynn Thomas, of Ace Irrigation, Kearney, has been selected as Small Businessman of the Year for the state of Nebraska, Norman Otto, regional director of Small Business Administration, Omaha, announced today.

"Mr. Thomas was chosen by SBA," Mr. Otto said, "because he is an ideal example of the type of home - grown industry that can be developed in many Nebraska communities. Mr. Thomas and Ace Irrigation exemplify the true sense of the development of small business in a free enterprise system.

"Under Mr. Thomas' outstanding managerial capabilities, his company has developed in a few short years, from a very small firm to an important contributor to employment in the Kearney area.

Lynn Thomas

99

I am truly grateful for the many people who have touched my life. And any success is shared with them.

—World-Herald Photo.

Nicest tribute of all . . . Thomas gets admiration from Mrs. Thomas, Lynda and Mike, and a smooch from Lee Ann.

'Man of Year' Overcame Handicap

By Tom Allan
Omaha World-Herald Staff Writer

Kearney, Neb.—Federal and state officials and local business and professional men gave Lynn Thomas, 42, a standing ovation Thursday noon in the banquet room of the Hotel Fort Kearney.

It was a spontaneous tribute to the Buffalo County farm boy who climbed to success over obstacles that could have deterred a less stout-hearted man.

Formally it was an accolade to his being chosen Nebraska's Small Business Man of the Year by the Small business Administration.

Although he sat humbly during the rousing tribute, Mr. Thomas, a polio victim crippled from the waist down since the age of 5, stood tallest of them all.

He refused to take credit, instead sharing his success with "people who have touched my life." They included his father, Vern, 81; Beverly, his wife and "backbone"; Merle (Mac) McClemens, his sales manager and "my legs," and other friends and associates.

When he took ownership of the Ace Irrigation and Manufacturing Company in January of 1962, the work force included him and three employees. Sales totaled $290,000 at the end of the year.

Today, four years later, his pay roll is in excess of 35 employees and sales during 1967 are expected to exceed $1,500,000.

The booming company, located in Kearney's expanding industrial tract on the old bomber base, manufactures aluminum irrigation tubing. It is one of three companies in the United States making 12-inch tubes.

The product is shipped throughout Colorado, Wyoming, South Dakota, Kansas and Missouri as well as throughout irrigation-minded Nebraska.

Ron Bycroft of Gibbon, his banker and friend, said one Mr. Thomas's codes of life has been: "No matter how bad off you think you are or how tough the old world is, you can always find another who is worse off than you."

Another philosophy has been setting goals and attaining them despite all obstacles.

As a boy, unable to participate in sports, Mr. Thomas set a goal of raising prize pigeons. A few years later he became Kearney's champion pigeon raiser.

Dick Dyer, President of the Kearney Chamber of Commerce and his former teacher, describing Mr. Thomas as a home-grown success," said: "When he was just an employee of the company he now owns he sat with his head going all the time thinking up ideas to make it a better company and when he took over he continued to think and work to make it better."

Norman Otto, Omaha regional SBA director, said Mr. Thomas was chosen as the state's SBA man of the Year because "he is an ideal example of the type of home-grown industry that can be developed in many Nebraska communities."

Mr. Otto added: "He and his company exemplify the true sense of the development of small business in the free enterprise system . . . The growth of his business is living proof to communities all over the state that the best source of new jobs and expanded industry is to give a helping hand to the men in their home town."

Mr. Thomas was given a gold key to the city by Kearney Mayor Francis Richards. He was lauded by Arnold Enders, executive of the neighboring Baldwin Manufacturing Company, for cooperation with employees and other businesses. Letters of commendation were received from Senators Carl Curtis and Roman Hruska and Representative Dave Martin.

This morning he and his family will be guests of honor at the Capitol in Lincoln where Gov. Norbert T. Tiemann will formally present him with the SBA award.

But perhaps none of the citations and praise will have meant as much to him as the adoration of his wife, son Mike, 11, and daughters Lynda, 14, and LeAnn, 10, as they clustered around after the ceremony—most especially that moment when LeAnn leaned over to give him a bear hug and a kiss. Another son, Dick, 6, didn't make the luncheon but is expected to make the trip to Lincoln this morning.

1968. Away we went. Things just kept getting better, making pipe and selling it.

Most farmers wanted six or eight-inch diameter pipe, but we got so were selling some ten and even some 12-inch diameter pipe to people.

I had ordered the tube mill to run four different sizes of pipe—6, 8, 10, and 12 inch diameter pipe. And I ordered it so it would run 0.0900 wall thickness, which was a thicker wall than the pipe produced by our competitors.

People asked, "What would you want 12 inch pipe for?" "And why would you need such a heavy wall pipe?"

"I don't know," I replied. "I think that maybe down the road there's a possibility that 12 inch pipe might become popular."

California Gold. Then about a year later, a company in California couldn't fulfill a big order for 12-inch diameter pipe. They had a machinists' strike, and they couldn't manufacture the pipe. And we were the only ones around, besides them, who made 12-inch pipe. So they called me up and ordered five miles of pipe. The order took seven flat railroad cars loaded with 45-foot lengths of 12-inch diameter pipe.

That was our first big order for pipe. We kept selling locally to the farmers. And we made a little money and we kept saving or investing it in inventory or equipment.

20 acres. Business went along really good, and we purchased the land under our buildings from the city. Then in 1969 Bob Caldwell wanted to sell a 20-acre piece of property situated just to the south of us. He wanted 40,000 dollars for it. So again, Ron went to bat for me, so we could borrow the money and buy that ground.

Ron got me the money to do all those things. And I owe a huge debt of gratitude to Ron for helping me on my way to showing a profit. Years later Ron backed Cimera Corporation, a new company making generators. Cimera went broke and Ron got stuck for half a million dollars, so that ruined Ron's banking career.

Ace Gate. We were making our own pipe, and I needed a good gate to sell with all the pipe we produced. I tried buying the Hastings gate from Hastings Irrigation, but they wouldn't sell any to us. They rightly looked at Ace Irrigation as competition, and they didn't want to help us in any way.

But I knew about an old style gate that never did sell for Rain Chief in Grand Island. It had a snap top similar to the Hastings gate, but it ran perpendicular to the pipe instead of horizontally. Nobody ever used it. I knew there was a possibility that the Hastings gate actually infringed on the patent for this gate.

Rain Chief went out of business years before, and the owner, Howard Sterns, retired to Buckeye, Arizona. So I called him up out there and asked him if he'd be willing to transfer that patent over to us.

He immediately responded. "Well, what'll you give me for it?"

I said, "I'll give you 200 dollars, and then I'll give you a penny for every gate we sell like that."

"You got yourself a deal," Howard replied.

Then I turned my attention to getting the gate manufactured. I called up Jerry Kroeker, who by that time was running Epp Irrigation in Henderson. They were making what they call a key hole gate. I had him make dies for a two cavity top and a two cavity bottom on the insert, and two cavities for putting the rubber boot on. In the early seventies, Jerry called and wanted to sell us the dies he had to make that gate. Plus he had a couple eight-ounce machines for manufacturing the gates he'd sell us for 7000 dollars apiece. We bought it all, and now we are in the gate business! We called it the Ace gate.

U.S. Marshall, Bob Kuteck. Then, one day a U.S. Marshal comes into the office and serves us with a lawsuit from Hastings Irrigation saying we are copying their gate. But I happened to know that when they did their patent search for the Hastings gate, they had left out my Rain Chief gate, which had a snap similar to the Hastings gate. My guess is if they had included it, then they couldn't have gotten a patent on their gate since it had a similar latch as my Rain Chief gate.

Now I needed an attorney to defend my gate. I drove over to visit Dick Dyer, an attorney in Kearney, who also was my seventh grade geography teacher before the war. I showed Dick the lawsuit and told him the whole story about my gate. He suggested I go to Bob Kuteck, an attorney in Omaha who did some work in patents.

So I made contact with Bob, and he had a small law firm called Kuteck, Rock and Campbell. Eventually their company would grow to be one of the larger law firms in the state of Nebraska. Bob and I hit it off really good, and I explained the situation and told him about the patent we had on this old gate. It cost me 12 grand to hire him on this deal. They did some research and found, indeed, that Hastings had neglected to include this gate that I now owned in their patent search. In their lawsuit, Hastings Irrigation was going to sue me for so much a gate, and they'd estimated how many gates.   It would've amounted to a lot of money.

It came out that we didn't even go to trial, because our two attorneys agreed that their gate infringed on this patent I owned! Hastings dropped the charges. Kuteck told me that we could have sued them for three cents a gate for every gate they ever made like that. But we just agreed that they would drop their lawsuit, and we wouldn't sue them for infringing on the patent we owned.

In the weeds.   By this time we were into installing underground pipe. Sometimes we would have two or three crews working. Als Fitzgerald, the lead foreman on these jobs, came to me and said that we couldn't find one of our trailers.

He told everyone, "Lynn sold the trailer and forgot he sold it."

Several years later, one of our dealers asked if we had lost one of our trailers.

"There's a trailer that looks like yours, sitting in a field north of Elm Creek," He said.

We went out and looked at it, and sure enough, it was our long lost trailer sitting there in the weeds. With all the hectic times of running the crews, Al forgot where it was.

PVC & MORE

The offer. In the early '70s, I almost sold the business. At that time, Lyndsay Manufacturing approached me and wanted to buy me out. Lyndsay built Zimmatic center pivots. They came down and went through our operation. They offered me a million four for the company, and I said I wanted a million five. They turned me down.   That was April 30, 1973.

Center pivots. Valley Irrigation had 18 counties in central Nebraska that were open for dealership. We applied and succeeded in getting the dealership on those 18 counties for center pivots. And the center pivot business started going good about that time. Along with the gated pipe, we made some money on that.

Then in the fall of 1973, Carmen Irrigation from Pleasanton sold us their pivot business. We hired some of their employees too. One was Norman Metz, who is still with our company today. Norm has taken on any job I've asked him to do.

 When we decided to get out of the center pivot business, I tried to sell the pivot parts back to Valley Irrigation. But they wanted to charge me a 15 percent restocking fee on all the parts. So I took out big ads in the Omaha World Herald and the Denver Post that announced:

Ex-Valley Pivot Dealer – Parts at 50% Off

Phone: 308-237-5173

By almost 10 am I had sold 50,000 dollars worth of parts.

Valley Pivot Company was very strict about only their dealers selling their parts. It seems Valley dealers called the factory and complained about our ads selling Valley parts. About 10:00 am the Vice President of Valley called and asked, "What are you doing, selling those Valley parts to the public?!"

I said, "You wanted to charge us a 15% restocking fee, and I refused. I want what we paid for the parts."

"Hold off 'til noon," he said, "and I'll get back to you."

He called back and said, "Call off your sale. We'll pay you full price."

PVC Pipe. In the mean time, I wanted to get into something more that correlated with irrigation and manufacturing. I thought of PVC pipe, which is constructed out of poly vinyl chloride. People didn't want to use asbestos pipe anymore, so PVC pipe was gaining in popularity. We already sold quite a bit of PVC pipe to customers, but we were the middleman, buying the pipe from one company and reselling it to our customers. Manufacturing PVC pipe would be a good fit with our irrigation business and aluminum pipe manufacturing.

So I set out to get into the PVC pipe business. Funding for such adventures could always prove to be interesting.

A New Bank. About this time Dean Halleck, the president of the Gibbon Exchange Bank paid me a visit. We were into them for about a half million dollars in loans at the time. Dean told me that our needs were too much for them and he just couldn't carry our line of credit any more.

"We really appreciate doing business with you," Dean said, "but you need to find a different bank than us."

Also during this time, I found out that I could get a loan for the PVC extruders through the Small Business Administration. So I filled out the paper work for that loan application and gave it to a banker at a Kearney bank for administrating. Then I went ahead and ordered two PVC extruders along with other supplies for manufacturing PVC pipe. But then I found out that the banker at the Kearney bank dropped the ball and left my SBA loan application papers sitting on his desk. The SBA loan opportunity evaporated while those papers sat there gathering dust.

Now I really needed a new bank!

I called Bob Kuteck, the patent attorney from Omaha who handled the dispute over the Ace gate. Bob and I had gotten along really well and became quick friends. We talked periodically, so I called him to talk about my banking situation, hoping to get a little perspective to help me figure out the best solution.

I described my predicament to Bob, and he piped up right away. "It's time you got away from small town banking anyway," he said. "Bring your paper work down to Omaha, and I'll introduce you to the president at the Omaha National Bank."

I drove down to Omaha and laid out my story to Mr. Snow, the Omaha National Bank president. Mr. Snow listened intently to my story and looked over my financials. He agreed to back me. In short order, though, they transferred us to a local, corresponding bank in Kearney, the Platte Valley State Bank.

At that time Bob Walker was president. Bob was a good banker, and once a person banked with him, he was quite a back slapper and really cared about a person. Bob and I got along great.

Financially, of most pressing concern were the two plastic extruders I ordered. They were going to cost over 400 grand just for the equipment. I went to Bob and he got the money for me to buy those machines.

Also in 1972 we needed more room, so we built a 20,000 square foot cement block building. We put the two PVC machines in the east side of that new building.

Up and Running. Our machines were called single screw extruders. A screw extruder has a long auger screw that fills the opening of a steel tube. Plastic powder is poured in at one end of the screw and mixed and melted as the screw turns. One machine ran six inch pipe and smaller, and one ran eight, ten and 12 inch pipe.

Once we started them up, we had to run them 24 hours a day. We couldn't shut them down because if we did, we'd have to restring the pipe, and it was hard to get the OD and the wall thickness just right. Once we got it right, we wanted to keep going as much as we could. So we would run 24 hours a day. I had two of my old time employees—Harold May and Norm Metz—who had worked for me for several years split the time into two 12 hour shifts. One worked the day shift from 12 noon to 12 midnight, and the other worked midnight to noon. Then we hired a bunch of college kids to work four-hour shifts. We ran PVC ten days straight, then we'd shut down for four days. That worked out pretty good, and our PVC pipe manufacturing got to rolling along pretty good.

PVC Compound Problems.   Our machines could eat a lot of powder compound in a 24-hour period. And there weren't too many people making the compound that we used to manufacture PVC pipe. We bought a little of our compound from Diamond Shamrock, but they had a low amount on how much compound we could buy from them. We bought the majority of our compound from Allied Chemical.

About six months after we started making PVC pipe, the salesman for Allied chemical came in for a visit. He stopped by periodically, so it was not a big surprise to see him walk in the office.

 But he sat down heavily in the chair across from my desk. "I'm sorry to tell you this," he said, "but the first of the year we are discontinuing the compound you are using to run your PVC pipe."

In shock, I glared at the salesman. Holy Christ!   That really put me in a bind! I just invested almost half million dollars in this machinery, and now I wouldn't have any compound to run them?

I was very upset and very angry, trying to figure out how in the heck I was going to make this thing work. There was just no way to get another supplier for the amounts we needed. I thought about it for a couple days, and then one night I went to bed with it on my mind. I woke up the next morning, and somehow my subconscious mind had worked on the problem.

My first thought that morning was: "Why don't you call the president of Allied Chemical and see if you can buy a couple million pounds before they stop running that compound?"

I went to the office that morning, and I did exactly what my subconscious told me to do. I boldly called up Allied Chemical and asked for the president.

Surprisingly, they put me right through to him. Unbelievable and unheard of that I could talk with him right then, no questions asked. I sat a little stunned, but there he was on the line with me.   So I explained my circumstances to him, saying that I'd just bought these high priced mills, and I didn't have another supplier.

"Do you suppose it would be possible for me to order a couple million pounds of this material before you shut it down?"

In the long silent pause after my question, I imagined him on the other end chewing on a cigar just as I chewed nervously on a cigar at my end.

Finally, he said, "Sure, we'll get your order filled before we shut down production."

So we made a deal.

By this time I was banking with Bob Walker at Platte Valley Bank. I went to Bob and explained the situation. I looked him straight in the eye and said matter-of-factly, "I need to buy two million pounds of powder from Allied Chemical. So I need about 325,000 dollars."

Bob looked back at me with a half smile and didn't blink an eye. "Ok, Lynn."

So we bought two million pounds of powder at 16 cents a pound. We got the quantity in, and we had that building full of powder. It was in 50-pound bags on pallets, and it was everywhere—every corner, every square foot that could hold a pallet, had a pallet sitting on it.

Luck: preparation meets opportunity

PVC demand. About this time, demand for PVC pipe grew immensely, and people were just clamoring for PVC underground pipe. And by the time Spring rolled around, the compound price had shot up exponentially.   In no time, there became a real shortage of the compound for making PVC pipe. And lucky us, here we sit with two million pounds of material and had all kinds of people wanting to buy from us. At the time, we probably had the largest stockpile of compound in the US!

I had a guy from Amarillo Texas, pleading with me in his friendly southern drawl. "If you'll sell me eight loads of eight inch PVC pipe, I'll give you half my business for the rest of my life." I knew that kind of commitment would be impossible for him to fulfill. And I didn't go for it. But he is a good example of just how desperate people were for PVC pipe. And besides, we had quite a few dealers spread out over three states, and I had customers here locally that wanted pipe.

I came up with a workable solution for selling pipe. I told my dealers and others: "I will sell you as many pounds of compound as you want at the present market value plus the manufacturing costs and our profit. But if you want it guaranteed, you've got to pay for it up front. Then when you need the pipe, we'll manufacture it to your specifications."

Well, we had money coming out of everybody's pocket wanting that kind of deal. And we ran those mills continuously. As a result, we had really great years in 1974 and 1975. We paid off our loan for the powder and still had a million in CDs in the Platte Valley Bank. And I realized at the time just how much the conscious mind feeds the subconscious mind so it can process the problem into a workable solution. Years ago on that morning when I woke up with the answer to the PVC compound problem, I knew the answer came from a place outside myself.

As time went on the demand for PVC decreased some. And the big boys like the Johns Manville Company out in Colorado cut the price down so low that we couldn't compete and make any money anymore. And we had sold all our original powder anyway. So we cut back on running pipe, and that way we'd at least have some for sale. We ran that way for a while, but finally business with PVC just quit.

But we were still in the irrigation business, and life was good.

We put out a lot of PVC pipe and we made some big money. We made enough money to build a 37,500-square-foot cement block building addition. We took 7,500 square feet of that building and put in new office space with a roomy display floor. We put the other 30,000 square feet into manufacturing space, giving us a whole new manufacturing plant. By the time we paid 500,000 dollars in income tax and paid another 500,000 dollars for the building and offices, we'd spent most the profits from the PVC.

I wanted to spend some time giving back to my community, so I ran for County Board of Supervisors.

County Board of Supervisors.

By 1974 I had some great people in the office, including Tom Bokenkamp, Lloyd Wilke and Mac McClemens. I knew I could trust them to run the daily operation of the company. And I wanted to spend some time giving back to my community and giving of myself. So I ran for the Buffalo County Board of Supervisors. The community voted for me by a large majority over an incumbent.

But it got tough being a new member, for on the board was a gentleman who had been on the board for 16 years, and he ruled with an iron arm. We didn't see eye to eye on many things and clashed often. In fact, he called for a meeting to reprimand me for being for term limits.

He called for a closed meeting; I objected and said, "If you're going to reprimand me, it will be in an open meeting."

On the day of the meeting, a large crowd came. "Mr. Big" told the public that I had a chip on my shoulder. I retaliated that it was not a chip, but a large log. As time went on, Mr. Big moved out of his district and had to resign.

I did not intend to run for a second term, but people came to me and said that I needed to stay on the board. Jack Lederman, A Democrat, asked me to stay on the board, even if it meant I just sit there and did nothing. So I went ahead and ran. No one ran against me. Then I decided if I was going to stay, this board needed someone with accounting experience. I persuaded Harry Pagels to run. Another man ran against him and won the seat. Harry's opponent knew I backed Harry, and he proceeded to be harder to get along with than the preceding Mr.Big!

I stayed on the board one year but into my second year, I resigned. Don't get me wrong, there were some great people on the board, like Dale Wright from Elm Creek, and Dorleen Weed just to name a couple outstanding people I served with. It was a traumatic time, but I wouldn't change it for anything.

One thing that came out of being on the Board was my continued friendship with attorney, Jim Knapp.

A couple years before I served on the Board, Jim called me one night and said, "Lynn, I need your help."

Jim went on to explain. "The Democratic nominee for President is coming to Kearney tomorrow morning, and I need a factory to take him through. Mr. Baldwin turned me down, and I'm in trouble."

I said, "Jim, you know I'm a Republican and can't in good conscience do that."

The democratic nominee was George McGovern.

"You think it over," he said, "and I'll call you in the morning."

Low and behold, the next morning I turned on the local radio station just in time to hear the broadcaster announce that the Democratic Nominee would tour Ace Irrigation that afternoon! Well, of course this was a surprise to me.

Later, I joked with Jim and said, "I'll get even with you for this!"

Sure enough, in due time I got into a disagreement with the County Sheriff at that time over some books he ordered. The Board agreed with me and turned down paying for the books. Then the Sheriff sued the Board for not paying for the books.

I called Jim Knapp and said, "Here's the story: the Board is being sued by the Sheriff, and I believe you owe me one. You will represent the County at no cost."

Jim agreed. We won. And Jim just sat back and smiled. Case closed.

Beverly and I met Ronald Reagan at a fundraiser in Grand Island before he became President of the United States.

Banking. Over the years I banked with several area banks. First I was with First National Bank and Harold Oldfather. Then I worked with Ron Bycroft, President at the Gibbon Exchange Bank. Next I went to Platte Valley State Bank for a number of good years. First off Bob Walker was President, and then later it was Norm Schmidt. For loan officers I dealt with Bill Richardson and Ron Bielenburg. And I got along fine with all these people.

Problems happened when the Platte Valley board of directors wanted to get the bank ready for sale. They brought in a "throat cutter" to work on getting the bank to look good for buyers. I call him a throat cutter, because this guy's methods literally cut the throats of local businesses. He made it so hard for me to operate that I nearly lost the business.

I'll never forget one repeating argument with him whereby he insisted: "If you need money to pay your bills, sell the inventory."

So finally I did sell inventory. I sold 100,000 dollars of aluminum coil. Then the following summer, I had to buy the same coil for 150,000 dollars.

In 1989 this brought me in contact with Dean Sach, President of York State Bank, York Ne. Dean held the mortgage for a company with some equipment in Henderson, and we became friends when I helped him sell that equipment.

When I told him of my troubles at the Kearney bank, he said, "You don't have to put up with that! I'll bank your needs."

Dean paid off the notes at Platte Valley State Bank, and then we set up new notes for the company. And he set me up with a great line of credit! From that day forward, our company thrived.

So the conclusion here is that the bank not loaning me money locally, pushed me to make the change to York State Bank.

Culvert. For several years I looked around for something to expand the business, something that would fit well with the irrigation manufacturing. Then one day in 1981 I found out about Eaton Metals, a company for sale in Omaha. They made grain bins and they made culvert pipe. I wasn't interested in the grain bin part of it, but the culvert aspect looked very interesting.

I made an appointment to visit with them on Friday the 13th of March 1981. I got there at nine o'clock in the morning and I met with the manager of the company. The owners decided the night before that they would sell the culvert division separate from the grain bin business. And whoever got the money there first, bought the culvert division. So I was pretty excited inside, but I didn't let them know. We went around and looked at the culvert division, and it was just perfect. It was just what I'd been looking for for a long time to match up with our irrigation part of the business.

So I went back to the office at Eaton Metals and made a phone call. By this time Norm Schmidt was president of Platte Valley Bank. I'd gotten along well with Norm, as well as I'd gotten along with Bob Walker. They were good bankers to deal with. So I told Norm the situation.

"Norm, I've found a culvert company I want to buy in Omaha. I need you to wire earnest money to their bank right away so I can seal this deal up. They want 10,000 dollars down on this deal right now, but the total price will be about 400,000 dollars."

"Are you sure that's what you want to do?"

I said, "Oh yea, this is a perfect match with our business!"

So Norm wired the money that morning, and just like that, we were in the culvert business. We ran the business from Omaha for a while. I sent Norm Metz and Kirt Noller down to run the business until we could move it to Kearney. We moved it to Kearney in October that year. We made the culvert division a subsidiary of Ace Irrigation and named it Ace/Eaton Metals. So that's the story of the beginning of the culvert division, Ace/Eaton Metals.

And it has been good to us.

*Above: Cover photo of Central States Industrial
Journal, October 1994*

*Article: "Diversification to culvert pipe ups Ace
Irrigation's sales 37 percent"*

Our company took a big hit during the agriculture recession of the '80s. But we climbed out of that hole, and the culvert division helped a lot with that. Culvert doesn't make the profit that irrigation or PVC did, but it had the volume so we could keep employees busy. We got to hiring more and more full time people again.

The culvert division continues to grow. In 2000 we built another 12,000 square foot building for culvert production. Then in 2004 we purchased a larger culvert mill, and now we can make pipe as large as 12 feet in diameter. In 2012 we purchased a sheet mill for the culvert division, and we also built another 15,000 square feet addition.

Our culvert is now sold throughout the Midwest to cities, counties, state and federal entities, private contractors and wholesalers for road and highway construction.

Diversify and expand. Over the years we expanded some areas of our business, and we diversified into other areas that fit well for us. Our diversification is part of the key that insures what looks to be a very bright future.

We are the midwest warehouse for Fresno Valves and Castings Inc., makers of irrigation valves and gates, filters and brass castings, and for Specified Fittings, makers of large-diameter plastic fittings.

In 1995 we bought equipment to do our own powder coating. At the time we had difficulty getting our powder coating done consistently by other companies when we needed it. So we decided to do our own. Word quickly spread that we do powder coating, and soon the powder coating aspect expanded into a small division of its own. Along with doing our own powder coating, we now do powder coating for other companies, metal artists, car and tractor restorers, and a multitude of other situations where powder coating is needed.

We run 12 injection-molding machines, which are used to manufacture mainly gates and a wide variety of gaskets. We retired the Ace gate years ago, but that gate holds many memories of the past, including the lawsuit for patent infringement and our victorious outcome.

We have shipped products throughout the USA and to Canada. Today we can have several culvert loads leaving daily. Our quick access to Interstate 80 has been a great asset in delivering products to our customers.

1952-2012

60th Anniversary

Concluding thoughts. From the day I started at Ace Irrigation to this day, I am above all a stickler for cost-conscious decision making at the company. And every employee is taught from day one to be cost conscious and encouraged to watch for ways to save on materials and product.

Today we have over 50 wonderful employees. Many employees have been with the company for more ten years, and there are a number of employees who have been here more than 25 years and some for over 40 years!.   Three of my kids, Lynda, Mike and Dick have been here for a long time. My daughter, LeAnn, works here now, and one of our projects has been to put this book together.

It has been and always will be about the people in my life. I had so many people encourage me and guide me and believe in me.

 Many thanks to these wonderful people:

To Professor Stretch Welch who taught me that "figures don't lie but liars figure."

To George Sobotka, the smartest businessman I ever knew, despite only going to eighth grade.

To Asa Gallup and Sam Porter who put together a plan that allowed me to buy Ace Irrigation—with absolutely no money.

To Bob Rapp (Norton Kansas) who had faith in me to advance me $15,000 every January for four years for future purchases back in 1963.

To Ron Bycroft (at the time the President of Gibbon Exchange Bank) who somehow helped us get the money so we could manufacture aluminum pipe.

To Bob Walker, President of Platte Valley State Bank 1973, who loaned us the money to buy the equipment to manufacture PVC pipe.

To Dean Sack and Bruce Riddell (York State Bank) in 1991 who had faith in us to finance our operation; and to them we owe a great deal of gratitude, for they allowed us to grow and prosper in the 1990s.

To Tom Bokenkamp and all the loyal employees who had faith to stay with the company.

To all our farmer friends, contractors and County Highway Departments who purchase our products over the years to allow us to prosper.

I must give credit. It behooves me to think I did all of this alone, for you need to surround yourself with loyal and caring people to have any success; one does not go through life without these people. In that vein I must give credit to family.

To my mother and dad who only had an eighth grade education, but raised nine children. They allowed me to be whatever I could be, even though they could see nothing but hardship for me, walking on crutches for the rest of my life.

To the kid's mother, Beverly, who allowed me to plow the profits back into the company instead of pushing to spend everything on a lavish living.

To my daughter Lynda, the one who always has an open heart to listen to our employees problems and brings them to me.

To my son Mike, who took over running the irrigation part of the business.

To my son Dick, whose inventive mind created many items that were important to our growth.

To Tom Bokenkamp, who is like my 5th child; he stood by me through thick and thin, and he took over running the culvert part of the business.

And to my daughter LeAnn, who pushed me to write this book; I could not have done it without her.

Dick, Mike, Lynda & LeAnn with me

No more crutches.   All my life I struggled some with my crutches on ice. If a crutch slides on the ice, it tilts the whole body and makes it nearly impossible to correct the imbalance. On an icy winter day back in 1985, I went to the Buffalo County Court House. I slipped on the ice outside the courthouse and took quite a fall. By the time my body mended, my shoulders and arms were too weak for me to get back up on crutches. Quite simply, my shoulders were worn out from a lifetime of carrying my full body weight.

So I switched to a wheelchair. I always knew that someday I'd need a wheelchair. Matter of fact, when I built the office addition back in the 70s, I also built a wheelchair accessible apartment for me adjacent to the office.   Living in that apartment makes it very handy for me to go to work. I open the metal door that divides the two spaces, and I can instantly be at home or the office!

Ah! Success, what is it? Dreams. To see your dreams come to life. To live long enough to enjoy your dreams and see your children and grand children mature and grow. To see employees come to life and join in your dreams of building a company that would eventually fulfill some of their dreams too. To feel comfortable in your own skin. To feel compassion for your fellow men and women, to want success for all.

I wish you success in your dreams, whatever they may be. Believe. Even if you think they might be pipe dreams.

Epilogue

An amazing life story like this needs some sort of conclusion or profound ending. The fact is, though, that Dad's story continues today, and well, there is no real ending to the story. But we still need to have some closing words—to share with you, the reader—a bit about his life today and some closing thoughts.

As I reflect back on Dad's life I notice a reoccurring theme that somehow, someway, he always managed. On crutches he managed to run away from the hospital in Lincoln and make it home to see his family. In school he managed his lessons while standing at a desk since the student desks didn't accommodate his braces. He managed to drive a car, truck and even a tractor, all the while perfecting the multi-step process of braking and shifting gears. He even managed to pull himself into Ron's airplane for a ride to visit the bankers in Omaha.

This find-a-way attitude carried over into his business perspective. When he needed something done, he found a way. When he needed compound for the new PVC extruders, he found a way. When he needed to make a delivery to Kansas on the 4th of July, he found a way. A thousand opportunities to give up and give in to obstacles—physical and otherwise—but he found a way.

Years ago it was a multi-step process for him to push the brakes in a car. Today, physically, it is a multi-step process for him to simply get into bed. It requires a board to slide on, and he has rings hanging above his bed, like gymnast rings, for him to grab and pull his body into a comfortable position. There are other physical challenges as well. Known as Post Polio Syndrome, some new physical problems show up years later in polio victims. But he perseveres.

And he never complains. Never. Matter of fact, he gets a little impatient with anyone who says anything about how much of a physical struggle life must be for him.

He literally ignores the struggle. He has an attitude that this is just part of life, and that's how it is. Physical struggles have always been there, but to have them continue to increase these many years later could discourage the most courageous of men. But he takes it all in stride and refuses to talk about it, putting it on the bottom of the list of things to talk about in the book.

As you have just witnessed by reading his story, he has the most amazing crack memory. It knocks me over that he can remember the first and last names of every kid in his third grade class. Or that he can remember the names of the owners of Kearney Livestock from 70 years ago. Or that he can remember the exact date and time that he went to Omaha over 20 years ago to buy a culvert mill. You read the story. You know. This is an amazing memory for detail!

He continues to be very active in the business. He works at his desk in the office every weekday, and he also works every Saturday as well in the irrigation busy season. And every day he rolls out into the plant and yards, checking on the progress of this or that or chatting with an employee about a current project.

And he still uses a manual wheel chair. He believes strongly in getting all the physical exercise possible, so he pushes himself all over the yards and manufacturing plant buildings.

Lynn Thomas is the hero to many people in this community and across the United States. And there's a reason for that attitude of respect and admiration—he has a good heart and soul.

He has the heart and soul of a survivor who appreciates life to the fullest, and he is a champion for second chances. It would take another book to tell about all the people he helped, all the projects in the community he supported, all the afternoons he simply gave an empathetic ear to a friend or stranger struggling with life.

But Dad is a humble man, and he would never let me write about all his accolades, all his community projects and assistance, and all the help he gave others. So we will leave it at that.

LeAnn Thomas

INDEX

LeAnn Thomas

LeAnn Thomas graduated magna cum laude from University of Montevallo, Montevallo Alabama with a Masters in Education and teaching certification in English, speech, journalism and drama. She taught at College of Southern Nevada in Nevada and at University of Nebraska at Kearney in Kearney, Nebraska.

LeAnn also enjoys art and worked on projects such as The Great Platte River Archway Monument in Kearney and the new Treasure Island in Las Vegas. She is working on a children's picture book based on a story Lynn made up and told her as a child.

She was born to Lynn and Beverly Thomas in Kearney, Nebraska. After living away from Nebraska for many years, she moved back to Kearney where she makes her home near her family, friends, and her roots.

Contact info and future plans

Lynn and LeAnn plan a hardback second edition of Pipe Dreams with even more local stories and adventures. They also plan an audio book whereby you will enjoy the story told in Lynn's own voice.

Feel free to contact Lynn or LeAnn at Ace Irrigation, 4740 East 39th Street, Kearney, Nebraska. The phone is 308-237-5173. Lynn also has a web site at WLynnThomas.com.